IMAGES
of America

HOOVER TOWER
AT STANFORD UNIVERSITY

As Stanford students, both Herbert Hoover, class of 1895, and his wife, Lou Henry Hoover, class of 1898, were influenced by the global outlook of the Stanford faculty. They both studied geology, traveled widely, and prior to World War I, they collected rare books on the history of international mining. With the outbreak of war, Herbert Hoover abandoned his business career and devoted his life to public service. His many years of experience as chairman of the Commission for Relief in Belgium (1914–1920), US food administrator (1917–1920), secretary of commerce (1921–1928), and US president (1929–1933) convinced him of the need for more research on the causes of war and peace. Although collecting began earlier, he officially founded his library collection in 1919 with a $50,000 commitment to fund the acquisition of primary documentation. The Hoovers are shown here in about 1928 at their home on the Stanford campus, which Lou began building in 1919 the same year as the founding of the Hoover War Library. (SHPC.)

On the Cover: The Hoover Tower at Stanford University has presided over the campus since 1941. It houses a vast and growing library of books and archives on the causes of war from 1900 to the present. Millions of visitors have enjoyed the view from the observation deck, and thousands of researchers have used the library for research. Hoover explained the mission of the Hoover Institution: "The purpose of this institution is to promote peace." (Courtesy Stanford News Service Historical Archives.)

IMAGES
of America

HOOVER TOWER AT STANFORD UNIVERSITY

Elena S. Danielson
Foreword by Eric T. Wakin

ARCADIA
PUBLISHING

ISBN 977-1-4671-2920-6

Published by Arcadia Publishing
Charleston, South Carolina

Printed in the United States of America

Library of Congress Control Number: 2017964137

For all general information, please contact Arcadia Publishing:
Telephone 843-853-2070
Fax 843-853-0044
E-mail sales@arcadiapublishing.com
For customer service and orders:
Toll-Free 1-888-313-2665

Visit us on the Internet at www.arcadiapublishing.com

To Ron, Erik, Mory, and Soren

Contents

Foreword

Herbert Hoover's unique contributions to preserving the historical record deserve to be more widely known and appreciated. My colleagues and I are delighted to partner with Arcadia Publishing to foster a deeper understanding of the scholarly side of the engineer, businessman, and humanitarian who became the 31st president of the United States. The Hoover Tower is a significant historical landmark in itself, but it—and its three surrounding buildings—are also home to the Hoover Institution on War, Revolution, and Peace, which was established as the Hoover War History Collection in 1919. Today, the Hoover Institution at Stanford University is unique in that it houses both an academic research center focused on public policy and a world-renowned library and archives.

For nearly a century, the Hoover Institution Library & Archives have been committed to collecting, preserving, and providing access to the world's most important material related to political, social, and economic change across the globe. The Hoover Institution Library & Archives have always been integral to the Hoover mission of "ideas defining a free society" and continue to support that mission through their collecting, workshops, fellowships, exhibitions, and digital projects. Their holdings in over 70 languages now make up one of the leading private scholarly research collections for studying the sweep of 20th and 21st century history.

The names of many donors on the walls inside the first floor of the Hoover Tower lobby speak to the great effort to fund its construction from 1939 to 1941. Today, a committed group of overseers ensures that the Hoover Institution has adequate resources to continue its work. The Hoover campus has expanded its space for scholars and collections with the 1967 Lou Henry Hoover Building; the 1978 Herbert Hoover Memorial Building; and, in 2017, the David and Joan Traitel Building.

The principles of individual, economic, and political freedom; private enterprise; and representative government were fundamental to the vision of Herbert Hoover, and the institution he founded continues to serve as a repository for the preservation and generation of knowledge and ideas, with the goal of improving the human condition.

—Eric T. Wakin, Deputy Director, Hoover Institution
Robert H. Malott Director, Hoover Library & Archives

ACKNOWLEDGMENTS

Eric T. Wakin and Jean McElwee Cannon of the Hoover Institution Library & Archives provided the impetus behind this book. The editors at Arcadia Publishing have been consistently helpful. This project was made possible by the extraordinary digital resources of the Stanford University Libraries, where innovative digitization has long been fostered by university librarian Michael Keller. I am indebted to Daniel Hartwig, university archivist, who facilitated the development of the Stanford Historical Photograph Collection, a database of over 16,000 images.

I received gracious assistance from many knowledgeable people, including Karen Bartholomew, Stanford Historical Society; Ronald Basic, research assistant; Rachel Bauer, formerly of the Hoover Institution Library & Archives; Jean McElwee Cannon, Hoover Institution Library & Archives; Jaime Fogel, Bok Tower Gardens, Lake Wales, Florida; Thomas W. Gilligan, the Tad and Dianne Taube Director of the Hoover Institution; Lindsey L. Givens, Arcadia Publishing; Charlotte Kwok Glasser, Stanford Historical Society; Daniel Hartwig, Stanford University archivist; Angel Hisnanick, Arcadia Publishing; Spencer Howard, Herbert Hoover Presidential Library, West Branch, Iowa; Vishnu Jani, Hoover Institution Library & Archives; Laura Jones, Stanford University archaeologist; Edward Kasinec, Visiting Fellow, Hoover Institution; Pamela Moreland, Stanford University News Service; Eisha Neely, Division of Rare and Manuscript Collections, Cornell University Library; Roxanne Nilan, former Stanford University archivist; Tim Edward Noakes, Department of Special Collections, Stanford University Library; Kyle Palermo, Hoover Institution; Miriam Palm, Stanford Historical Society; Tamar Ravid, Branner Earth Sciences Map Library; Josh Schneider, assistant university archivist, Stanford; Julie Sweetkind-Singer, head, Branner Earth Sciences Map Library & Map Collections; Chor Seng Tan, Stanford graduate student in materials science and engineering; Jeffrey T. Tilman, historian, University of Cincinnati; Paul V. Turner, Stanford University faculty, emeritus; Eric T. Wakin, deputy director of the Hoover Institution / Robert H. Malott Director of the Hoover Institution Library & Archives; and Craig G. Wright, Herbert Hoover Presidential Library, West Branch, Iowa.

For additional sources and acknowledgments, please consult stanford.academia.edu/ElenaDanielson.

Sources are indicated by the following acronyms:

Bancroft Library, University of California, Berkeley (BANC.)
Hoover Institution Library and Archives (HOOVER.)
Stanford Historical Photograph Collection (SHPC.)
Stanford University News Service (SUNS.)
Herbert Hoover Presidential Library, West Branch, Iowa (WESTBRANCH.)

Introduction

The Hoover Tower stands as a tangible symbol of Stanford University. The founders and pioneers of Stanford University and the builders of the library that is the Hoover Tower shared an idealistic vision that is surprisingly consistent from Sen. Leland Stanford's speech opening the university in 1891 to Herbert Hoover's speech dedicating the then new tower 50 years later in 1941. Stanford, who traveled widely in Germany and Russia in 1890, was concerned about the threat to peace posed by the large standing armies and civilian police forces he had seen. He saw research and education as essential remedies. Herbert Hoover, who, after graduating from Stanford, experienced war and social upheavals in China, Russia, and Europe, collected documentation on the causes of war, revolution, and peace. In 1941, as another world war was starting, he dedicated his library building "to promote peace." Some of the people who built up the library and archives in the tower are well known, such as former US president Herbert Hoover (1874–1964) himself and renowned architect Arthur Brown Jr. (1874–1957). Many of the key people involved are relatively unknown, such as collector and Stanford historian Ephraim Douglass Adams (1865–1930), founding curator and Stanford historian Ralph H. Lutz (1886–1968), Hoover's wife, Lou Henry Hoover (1874–1944), and third Stanford University president Ray Lyman Wilbur (1875–1949). They all had long histories with the enterprise of the university, going back to its early years. The first two university presidents, David Starr Jordan and John Casper Branner, were both avid book and manuscript collectors with broad international interests. Together, Jordan and Branner encouraged the teenaged student Herbert Hoover and the high spirited young woman he studied geology with, Lou Henry, to read and travel widely as they had done. Jordan and Branner were themselves following in the footsteps of Jordan's mentor the celebrated historian, diplomat, and bibliophile Andrew Dickson White (1832–1918), founding president of Cornell University and advisor to Sen. Leland Stanford (1824–1893) and Jane Stanford (1828–1905) on the plans for the university being built on their 8,000-acre Palo Alto Stock Farm, located 30 miles south of San Francisco. Jordan and Branner navigated the university through the financial crisis in 1893 when Leland Stanford's death led to crippling litigation that challenged the funding of the university and again through the crisis of 1906, when a devastating earthquake reduced much of the beautiful new sandstone architecture, including the 80-foot-tall bell tower on the church, to rubble. Herbert and Lou Henry Hoover, Ray Lyman Wilbur, and Ralph Lutz were all Stanford students who saw the perseverance of these leaders overcome major setbacks to build a world-class, innovative university. They were determined to contribute to the legacy of the founders. The Hoover Institution Library & Archives and its affiliated public policy center are the results of their shared vision.

One

Herbert Hoover and Stanford University 1891–1918

Why is the iconic Hoover Tower, with Herbert Hoover's library and archives on war and peace, located at Stanford University? In 1891, when Leland and Jane Stanford opened the university, Hoover was among the first to enroll in the pioneer class of 1895. He had just turned 17. Hoover's career and the university's path to eminence were equally unpredictable and closely intertwined. As a university trustee for half a century, Hoover was involved with the university's growth his entire adult life, and he helped navigate it through financial difficulties several times. The university's professoriate and his fellow students shaped his life and interests. Although residing in a then remote, rural ranching area of California, the pioneer faculty was highly cosmopolitan. A zoologist by training, the first president, David Starr Jordan, also had a strong interest in international relations and became a well-known peace advocate. He received two medals from Japan. Hoover's advisor, geologist John Casper Branner, was a leading expert on mineral-rich Brazil and encouraged his students to travel as he had done. Former Cornell president Andrew D. White shared his experiences as US minister to Germany and Imperial Russia with the early Stanford community. While considered shy, the boy Hoover forged lasting friendships with faculty and his fellow students. One lifetime friend was Ray Lyman Wilbur, class of 1896, third president of Stanford University, and Hoover's secretary of the interior during his presidential administration. Hoover married his other great friend, the bright and adventurous Lou Henry, Stanford class of 1898, soon after her graduation, and they eagerly left for China immediately after their wedding ceremony in 1899. As Stanford university president, Ray Lyman Wilbur would shepherd the development of the Hoover Library. With her strong interest in architecture, Lou Henry Hoover had suggestions for the tower as well. Both Lou Henry Hoover and Ray Lyman Wilbur were on campus in 1941 when Herbert Hoover inaugurated the newly constructed Hoover Tower 50 years after the opening of the university.

Originally known as the War Collection, the library would go through various name changes over the years: The Hoover War Library (1922), Hoover Library on War, Revolution and Peace (1938), Hoover Institute and Library on War, Revolution and Peace (1946), and finally, the Hoover Institution on War, Revolution and Peace (1957). The purpose remained the same: document-based research on policies that promote domestic freedom and international peace.

The newly constructed Hoover Tower was dedicated on June 20, 1941, as part of the 50th anniversary celebrations of the founding of Stanford University. The tower was built to preserve the records of World War I and soon would be needed to hold documentation on the looming global conflict, which was on everyone's mind at the time of the dedication. On the steps of the tower, in front of a crowd of distinguished academicians from all over the United States, Herbert Hoover dedicated the tower as a library and as a monument: "The purpose of this institution is to promote peace. Its records stand as a challenge to those who promote war. They should attract those who search for peace." (SHPC.)

On October 1, 1891, fifty years earlier, Leland and Jane Stanford dedicated the newly constructed Inner Quad of Stanford University, built of sandstone and tile in Richardsonian Romanesque style. The previous year, the Stanfords, who remembered the Civil War, had traveled through Germany and Imperial Russia, where they were alarmed by the large standing armies and police forces they witnessed. In his dedication remarks, Leland Stanford looked to education as the only remedy: "When we remember the possibilities of civilization and the power of education, we can foresee a time when these soldiers and policemen shall be changed to useful, producing citizens, engaged in lifting the burdens of the people instead of increasing them. . . . Education by teaching the intelligent use of machinery is the only remedy for such waste." The photograph shows the Stanfords under a portrait of their late son Leland Stanford Jr. On the right, shielded from the sun by an umbrella, is the first university president David Starr Jordan, a noted peace activist. Herbert Hoover at age 17 was present in the crowd. (SHPC.)

As a student, Hoover was shy but known for his determination and his loyalty to friends. An orphan from an orderly but impoverished Quaker family, his limited elementary education did not prepare him to pass Stanford's entrance examinations. He was admitted on condition of passing before graduation. While Stanford University was then tuition-free, Hoover still had to work odd jobs to pay room and board. (HOOVER.)

Encina Hall was completed as a dormitory just in time for the arrival of the pioneer class of students in 1891. Hoover was among the first students to move in. He later found less expensive lodging elsewhere. Fifty years later, Hoover would open his library immediately to the west of Encina Hall, which today houses offices and research groups such as the Freeman Spogli Institute for International Studies. (SHPC.)

As soon as the charismatic geologist John Casper Branner came to campus, Hoover changed his major from engineering to geology. Shown here in 1893, lower left, with his surveying equipment, he was sent by Branner to survey in Arkansas as well as the Sierras, often with the US Geological Survey. Hoover developed a love of travel and a love of technology that lasted the rest of his life. (HOOVER.)

Branner, seated center with a full beard, is shown surrounded by his geology students. Here, Herbert Hoover is standing, second from left. An ardent bibliophile, Branner hired Hoover to work as an assistant in his office, with its famous collection of rare mining books and journals. Hoover, who was assigned to have the incoming journals bound and shelved, developed a lifelong passion for books and libraries. (HOOVER.)

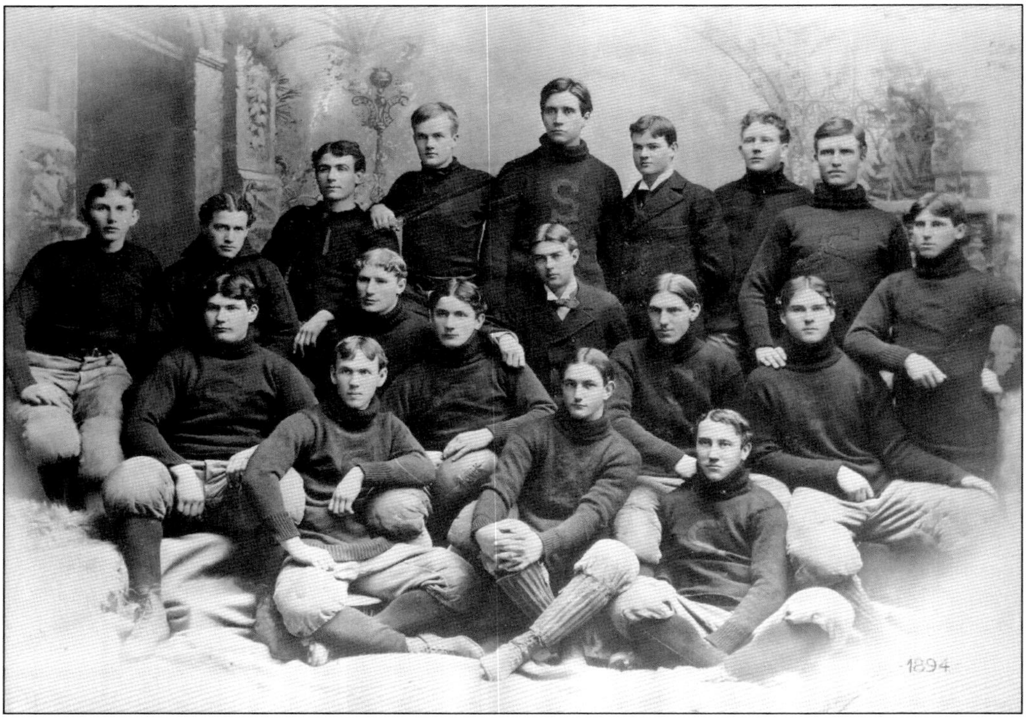

Seen here with the Stanford football team, back row fourth from the left, in 1894, Hoover was elected student body treasurer and worked to regularize the finances of the athletic programs, something neglected in the university's early years. Hoover honed his accounting skills with the US Geological Summer Survey. He was a spectator at the first Berkeley-Stanford game in 1892 as a freshman but did not have any official role. (HOOVER.)

A graduating senior in 1895, Hoover, center, still has a boyish look compared with the geology graduate students John Fletcher Newsom, left, and John H. Means, right. Newsom was much impressed with Hoover's work ethic. Geology professor John Casper Branner kept in touch with his students as they went out in the world. Hoover would go on to hire many Stanford students for challenging work in Australia, China, and Russia. (HOOVER.)

ZION, HOOVER, COLLINS.

We are the great triumvirate,
The awful Trinity of Fate.
On things scholastic or athletic
We speak with utterance prophetic.
This place, we Three, by love inspired,
Have scientifically wired ;
And so (our motives all the best)
When an election comes, with zest
We press the buttons and do the rest.

Hoover was successful in student politics. His 1895 class yearbook depicted him on the left in a photo-collage together with two of his political allies E.R. Zion and Samuel Collins as the invincible triumvirate, who have the campus wired and press buttons to make things work. By Hoover's hand is a sign identifying him as "manager." (Courtesy of the Department of Special Collections, Stanford University Libraries.)

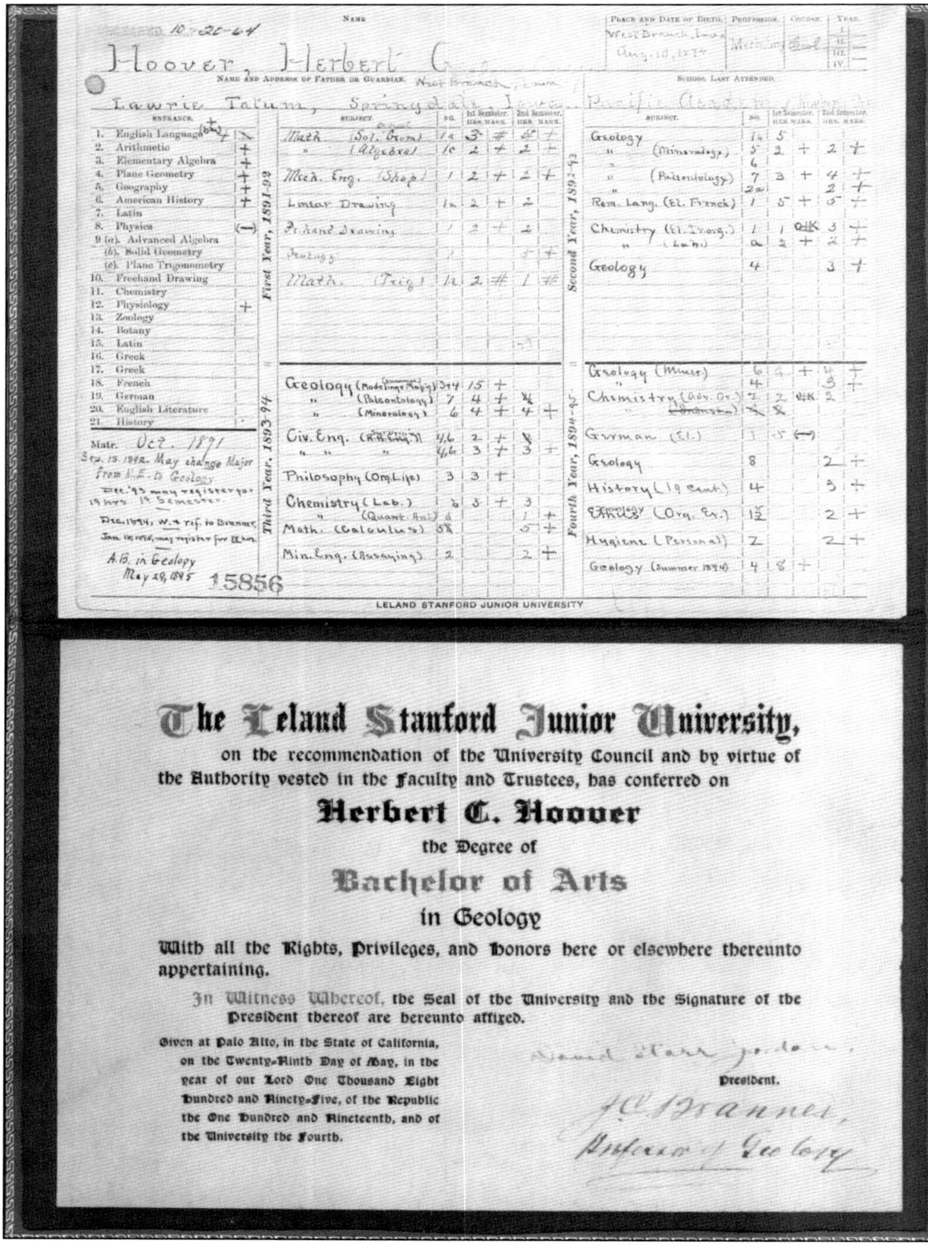

Hoover, Herbert C.

LELAND STANFORD JUNIOR UNIVERSITY

The Leland Stanford Junior University,
on the recommendation of the University Council and by virtue of the Authority vested in the Faculty and Trustees, has conferred on

Herbert C. Hoover

the Degree of

Bachelor of Arts

in Geology

With all the Rights, Privileges, and Honors here or elsewhere thereunto appertaining.

In Witness Whereof, the Seal of the University and the Signature of the President thereof are hereunto affixed.

Given at Palo Alto, in the State of California, on the Twenty-Ninth Day of May, in the year of our Lord One Thousand Eight Hundred and Ninety-five, of the Republic the One Hundred and Nineteenth, and of the University the Fourth.

David Starr Jordan, President.

J. C. Branner, Professor of Geology

Herbert Hoover's Stanford diploma was signed by both university president David Starr Jordan and his mentor, geology professor John Casper Branner. His transcript reflects his strength in technical subjects and somewhat less stellar performance in the humanities. In order to graduate on time, he had to pass the English requirement that he had failed on the entrance exam. His faculty and Lou Henry helped him overcome this last hurdle in his senior year. After graduation, Hoover consulted frequently with Jordan and Branner on career decisions, specifically whether to go into the risky field of international mining or stay in the safer employ of the US Geological Survey. They urged him to go for the more challenging option. He remained in close touch with them regarding university matters as his career gained traction. (HOOVER.)

Lou Henry was already a school teacher when she heard a lecture by Branner at San Jose Normal School and decided to study geology at Stanford, entering in Herbert's last year. Lou and Herbert soon had an understanding that they would get engaged once he had a well-paying job and she had finished her degree. Working in San Francisco, he would return to visit her and former faculty. (HOOVER.)

Sporty and adventurous, Lou Henry is seen here riding a donkey. She was an accomplished equestrian and loved camping and target shooting. Like her future husband, she had an affinity for science; unlike him, she had an affinity for learning languages. (SHPC.)

At a student picnic, Lou Henry poses in the center of the group with her geologist's pick, the symbol of her and Herbert Hoover's profession. (SHPC.)

Lou Henry's 1898 diploma is preserved in the Hoover Archives and has been on display in the Hoover Tower. In 1899 Hoover returned from a successful gold mining venture in Australia; they married at her parents' home in Monterey. The next day, they traveled to Tientsin, China, where he had a promising mining position, and she managed the paperwork in his office. (HOOVER.)

John Casper Branner encouraged both men and women to study geology. Lou Henry was the president of the geology club just as Herbert had been earlier. There were five women students in the geology club, according to the student yearbook. Branner helped both Lou and Herbert with their job searches after graduation. Once David Starr Jordan turned to peace activism full time, Hoover, by then a successful businessman, supported Branner as the second president of the university. Jordan became chancellor. (SHPC.)

Ray Lyman Wilbur (1875–1949) was a freshman in 1892 when he met Hoover, then a sophomore. They became lifelong friends. A natural leader, Wilbur served as senior class president. Once he had a substantial income in China, Hoover would anonymously send Wilbur financial support to help him through medical school. (SHPC.)

Ray Lyman Wilbur, third from the left, had a serious demeanor even while relaxing on a student field trip. With Hoover's support, Wilbur became the third university president (1916–1943) and also simultaneously secretary of the interior (1929–1933) in the Hoover Administration. In the latter role, he supervised the construction of Hoover Dam, and then later, back at Stanford, he presided over the construction of Hoover Tower (1939–1941). (SHPC.)

Jordan became president of Stanford at age 40 at the suggestion of Cornell's Andrew D. White. Both White and Jordan were concerned with preventing war. Jordan eventually gave up university administration to work full time for peace. He engaged Stanford undergraduate Ralph Lutz to help manage his extensive peace correspondence. Lutz eventually became a founding curator of the Hoover Archives, and Jordan's peace papers came to the Hoover Institution. (SHPC.)

A different side of President Jordan came out during events such as this baseball game accompanied by student "high jinx." Charles K. Field, class of 1895, used this picture in a slide show of 98 historical photographs projected on the sandstone wall of the Quad during the 50th anniversary celebrations in October 1941. The Quad was illuminated by mercury lights on the new tower. (SHPC.)

When the Hoover Tower was dedicated in 1941, friends of Jordan and Hoover acquired this bust of David Starr Jordan, by artist Elizabeth Norton, to display in the tower's inner lobby. Jordan saw the university through its two most challenging periods, in 1893 after Leland Stanford died and the university finances were challenged by litigation, and in 1906 after the earthquake severely damaged the university buildings. (SHPC.)

Jordan, who was awarded the "Order of the Sacred Treasure, Second Class," by Japanese emperor Meiji, encouraged Stanford historian Payson J. Treat to document the history of China, Japan, and Australia. By 1907, Hoover donated some $2,500, for Treat's acquisitions, when history books typically cost about $1 to $2 each. Hoover donated his own large collection of over 500 books on China to the Stanford University Library. (SHPC.)

The Hoovers lived in Tientsin, China, during the tumultuous era of the Boxer Rebellion, 1899–1901. Lou's physical courage enabled her to help others secure food and medical help during the bombardment. She is shown here in a weathered photograph by one of the large field artillery pieces. Their own house was damaged during the rebellion. (WESTBRANCH.)

Despite the dangers, the Hoovers thrived in China, where they studied the language and history. Hoover taught a class on mining at a local university with another former Branner student, N.F. Drake. Lou began to collect Chinese blue and white porcelain. Fine examples from the Hoover porcelain collection have been on display in the Hoover Tower for decades, as shown in this exhibition from the 1960s. (SUNS.)

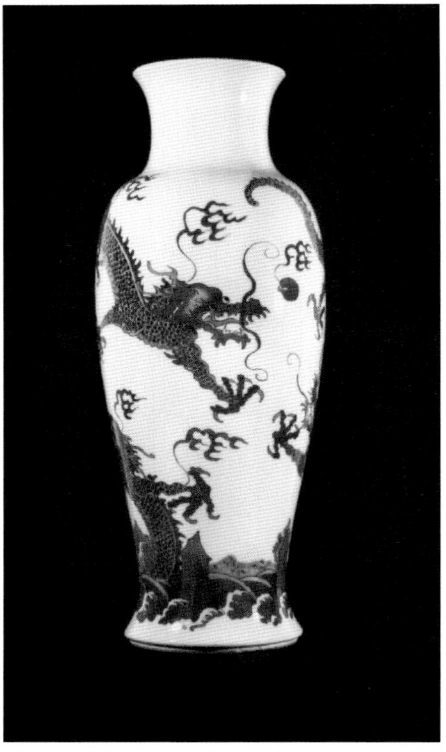

One of the Chinese vases often displayed in the Hoover Tower serves as a memento of Hoover's work as a mining engineer in China at the turn of the 20th century. He has been credited as the first to introduce large-scale Western technology into Chinese industrial production at the Kaiping coal mines. (HOOVER.)

Herbert Hoover continued collecting Chinese blue and white porcelain, even after Lou's death in 1944. According to his art dealer Frank Caro, Hoover was fascinated by the chemistry of porcelain and glazes and became a knowledgeable connoisseur. (SHPC.)

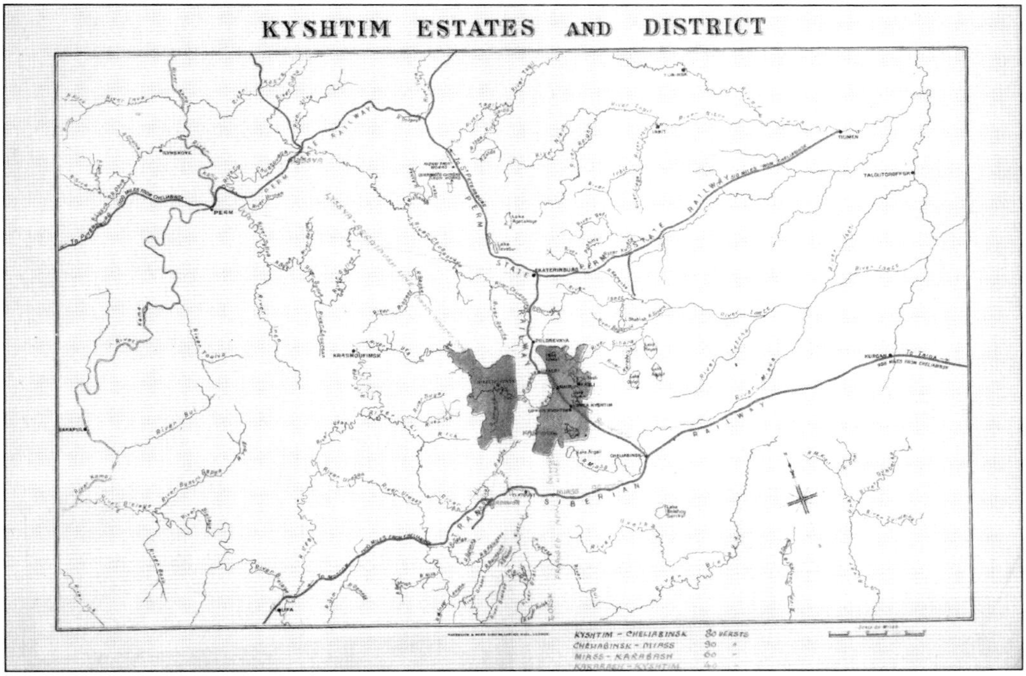

After leaving a British firm, Hoover began exploring opportunities in Imperial Russia. He invested in a copper and iron operation in a remote area of the Urals near Ekaterinburg, called Kyshtym, upgrading the equipment and improving profits. He made several trips to Russia between 1909 and 1913. Lou Henry Hoover often traveled with him. An emergency passport in the Hoover Archives documents her trip to Russia in 1913. (WESTBRANCH.)

A memento of his Russian experience, Hoover admired this sculpture of Leo Tolstoy, author of *War and Peace*. It was made in the Kyshtym region from Kasli iron according to a design by the artist A.A. Solovieva. Hoover read Andrew D. White's memoirs that describe conversations with Tolstoy. In 1939, Hoover became the honorary chairman of the Tolstoy Foundation in New York, a title he retained until his death in 1964. (HOOVER.)

Embroidered flour sacks such as this tell the story of Herbert Hoover's unprecedented humanitarian relief efforts in World War I. The invasion of Belgium by the German army so alarmed Hoover that he abandoned his mining career and turned to supplying food to the beleaguered civilian Belgian population. The American flour was baked into bread for the hungry children, and the empty sacks were decorated by the Belgian women. (HOOVER.)

Herbert Hoover's Commission for the Relief of Belgium generated huge enthusiasm among idealistic Americans and much interest among the Stanford community. Lou Henry Hoover, shown here on the right in a Belgian costume, joined in the fundraising events on campus with her usual energy. She raised enough money to launch an entire ship with food supplies for the starving, in support of her husband's agency. (SHPC.)

In addition to funding shipments of food to Belgium, Lou Henry Hoover provided marketing assistance for the Belgian lace makers so they could support themselves and their children during the war. Inspired by the American aid, the Belgian women often incorporated patriotic American motifs in their designs. Because of this, the Hoover Archives, dedicated to the study of war, revolution, and peace, preserves a collection of Belgian lace. (HOOVER.)

In an uncharacteristically glamorous dress, Lou Henry Hoover modeled a Belgian lace shawl. She dedicated the photograph to her friend the Vicomtesse de Beughem, an American (married to a Belgian aristocrat) who had helped her support the women making lace for sale during the German occupation of Belgium. (HOOVER.)

Stanford biology professor Vernon Kellogg (1867–1937) took a strong interest in the Commission for Relief in Belgium (CRB) and served among the army of volunteers to organize and distribute food relief in wartime. He would later serve in Hoover's organization to fight famine in post-revolutionary Russia. (SHPC.)

Copyright by Underwood & Underwood

HERBERT HOOVER

Chairman of the Commission for Relief in Belgium from the beginning to the present. Now also United States Food Administrator.

FIGHTING STARVATION IN BELGIUM

BY

VERNON KELLOGG

OF THE

COMMISSION FOR RELIEF IN BELGIUM

ILLUSTRATED

GARDEN CITY NEW YORK

DOUBLEDAY, PAGE & COMPANY

1918

Kellogg's history of the CRB remains a primary source on Hoover's groundbreaking program for international aid, a bold innovation at the time. (HOOVER.)

Another Stanford faculty member who took a strong interest in the Commission for Relief in Belgium was historian Ephraim Douglass Adams (1865–1930). Already firm friends, Adams had visited the Hoovers at their home in London in 1908 while he was conducting research on British-American relations. Hoover had provided Adams with $400 to obtain copies of historical diplomatic documents from the British Public Record Office. Adams described the Hoover home in London as filled with "books and books and books." In February 1915, Adams brought up the subject of donating the CRB papers to Stanford. On May 19, 1915, Adams again wrote to Hoover, "I anxiously hope that Stanford may someday have the historical records of the Belgian Relief Commission." (SHPC.)

Hoover repeatedly gave credit to Andrew Dickson White for the concept behind his library. A diplomat, historian, and first president of Cornell University, White had declined Leland Stanford's request to serve as first university president, but provided advice for building a nonsectarian, coeducational university. A great collector, White donated his photographs of architectural monuments to Cornell, with examples from the firm of H.H. Richardson. In 1891, White also donated his vast collection of original documents on the French Revolution to Cornell. These primary materials were the basis for the class he taught at Stanford in 1892 on the causes of the French Revolution. White donated a proclamation poster from the 1848 revolution in Europe to the Stanford Library. He was greatly concerned about instability in Russia and Europe. When Professor Adams urged Hoover to save his papers from the CRB for Stanford, collecting archival material and ephemeral posters on war and peace was already an idea that was in circulation among the early Stanford faculty and students. (Division of Rare and Manuscript Collections, Cornell University Library.)

Two

Founding the Hoover Library & Archives 1919–1939

During his business career, Herbert Hoover primarily lived abroad, but he considered Stanford his home base: "the best place in the world." He sent money to help friends such as Ray Lyman Wilbur and his own brother Theodore Hoover and the university library. As early as 1909, he supported the construction of an egalitarian student social hall, important to Hoover, who had been unable to afford to join a fraternity. Once he became a trustee, Hoover hired Bakewell and Brown to design the student union. Both Herbert and Lou Henry Hoover worked on fundraising over several years. The Stanford Union, completed in stages, was intended to "inoculate against the bacillus of social inequality." In donating both books and funding to the library, he specifically wanted to upgrade the international research collections, an interest he and Jordan shared. Originally, his library gifts were merged with the general university library holdings.

The Russian Revolution had a great impact on Hoover. He had traveled through Ekaterinburg in 1913 and witnessed firsthand the coexistence of a high level of culture and cruel inequality. Five years later, July 17, 1918, in the wake of the revolution, the tsar of Russia and his wife and children were murdered in Ekaterinburg. He wrote that preventing the spread of such anarchy was "the greatest problem that our government has ever faced." Hoover had a conceptual background to understand these events. Leland Stanford advocated education as a solution: "An intelligent system of education would correct this inequality. . . . It would achieve a bloodless revolution and establish a Republic of industry, merit and learning." Andrew D. White had lectured at Stanford in 1892 on the causes of the French Revolution, and White had watched events in Germany and Russia with alarm, writing about them in his memoirs, which Hoover had read. Documenting the causes of the Russian Revolution, in Hoover's view, could help prevent the spread of anarchy.

In 1919, Lou Henry Hoover built a home on land leased from Stanford University. That year, the university finally completed a library building. The architect was Arthur Brown Jr. Herbert Hoover's collections on war and peace would have their own dedicated space in the new building.

Herbert Hoover thrived on the emerging technology of his era. Newly expanded communications, such as ship to shore radio and long-distance telegraph lines, enabled him to coordinate his relief programs during World War I in chaotic conditions. Later, he would operate his own radio set in his campus home in the 1920s. At the onset of World War II, the tower housed a radio listening post. (WESTBRANCH.)

Both Lou Henry and Herbert Hoover enjoyed travel by train and ocean liner. He spent an estimated 100 weeks of his life, or two full years, circling the world five times before the era of aviation. He traveled the entire reach of the Trans-Siberian Railroad in 1909 from St. Petersburg to Korea and back. Here, the Hoovers are seen in their natural element, traveling by ship. (SHPC.)

As expatriate Americans abroad, the Hoovers brought their academic interests from Stanford along with them as they traveled. They translated a classic mining treatise from 1556, Georgius Agricola's *De Re Metallica,* from Latin into English. A close friend, Edgar Rickard, was entrusted with publishing the translation with full illustrations and a vellum binding in 1912. Rickard was later instrumental in securing funding for the construction of Hoover Tower. (HOOVER.)

Their translation work inspired them to collect rare volumes from the history of mining. By 1911, they were purchasing over 100 antique books annually. One of the oldest was *Ein nützlich Bergbüchlin.* The Hoovers acquired a copy from 1527 with delightful illustrations. Edgar Rickard commissioned a bookplate as a Christmas present for his friends and asked the artist to use one of the illustrations from this pamphlet. (HOOVER.)

Primarily living abroad in Australia, China, London, and Paris from 1897 to 1919, Herbert Hoover kept in close contact with Stanford University and friends in neighboring Palo Alto. A tall tree came to symbolize both the city and the university and is found on the university logo. Herbert and Lou Henry Hoover always considered their alma mater as their home base, where they would eventually return. (SHPC.)

Hoover gave lectures at Stanford in 1909, which he published as ***The Principles of Mining***. Remembering his years as an impoverished student, he also supported the construction of the Stanford Union, where all students including those who could not afford fraternity or sorority housing could socialize. With Hoover's generous support, the first phase was completed in 1915, and the final expansion was ready in 1922. (SHPC.)

As a Stanford trustee since 1912, Hoover was aware of the university's plans, begun in 1913, for a dedicated university library building, to be designed by the firm of Bakewell and Brown. The library had been in cramped quarters on the Quad. Although planning started in 1913, World War I delayed construction of the more spacious library, which was finally dedicated in 1919. (SHPC.)

The main west entrance to university library preserves the original architecture, now known as the Bing Wing. With a large extension on the east side of the building added in 1980, it continues to be the main library on campus, renamed the Cecil H. Green Library. (SHPC.)

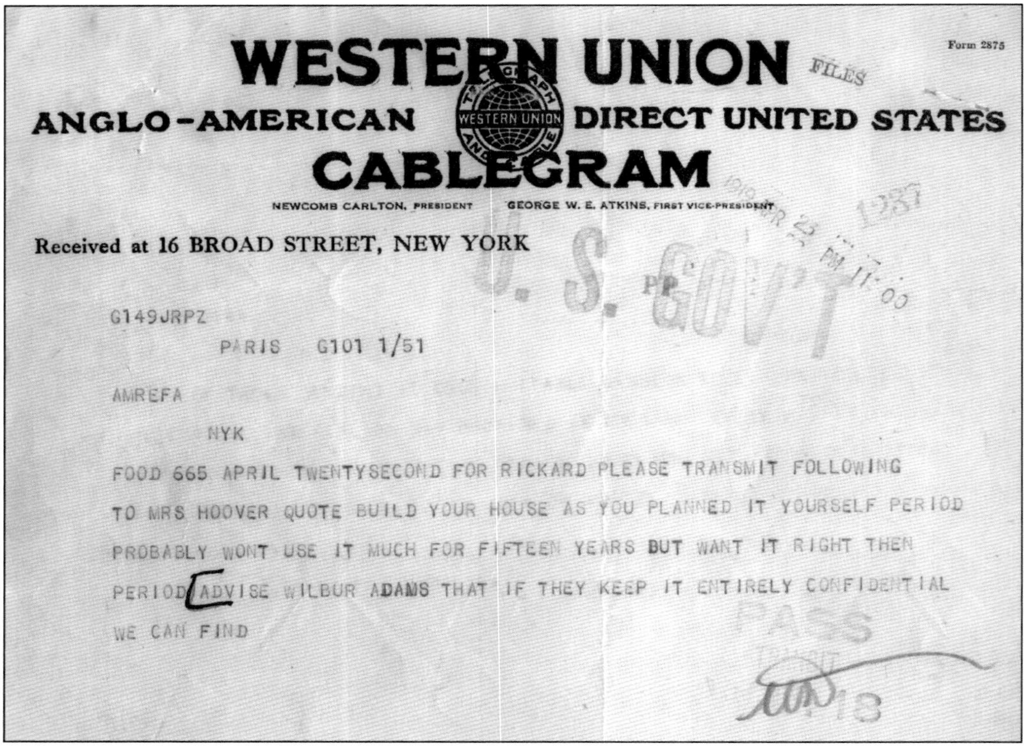

WESTERN UNION

ANGLO-AMERICAN DIRECT UNITED STATES

CABLEGRAM

NEWCOMB CARLTON, PRESIDENT GEORGE W. E. ATKINS, FIRST VICE-PRESIDENT

Received at 16 BROAD STREET, NEW YORK

G149JRPZ

PARIS G101 1/51

AMREFA

NYK

FOOD 665 APRIL TWENTYSECOND FOR RICKARD PLEASE TRANSMIT FOLLOWING TO MRS HOOVER QUOTE BUILD YOUR HOUSE AS YOU PLANNED IT YOURSELF PERIOD PROBABLY WONT USE IT MUCH FOR FIFTEEN YEARS BUT WANT IT RIGHT THEN PERIOD ADVISE WILBUR ADAMS THAT IF THEY KEEP IT ENTIRELY CONFIDENTIAL WE CAN FIND

Throughout his early career when he was constantly traveling, Hoover managed his complex business and humanitarian enterprises with daily barrages of cryptically succinct telegrams. One telegram from Paris to New York dated April 22, 1919, changed the face of Stanford forever. He first instructed his trusted assistant Edward Rickard to tell Lou Henry Hoover to "build your house as you planned it yourself" on campus, and he separately authorized, in strict confidence, funds not to exceed \$50,000, or \$700,000 in 2018 currency, to send a "mission to Europe to collect historical materials on war." With one two-page telegram, he established the foundations for an innovative archival library that would serve the scholarly community and for a beautiful home on campus that would eventually serve as the university president's residence—with one telegram, he established a home for the intellect and a home for the heart. (HOOVER.)

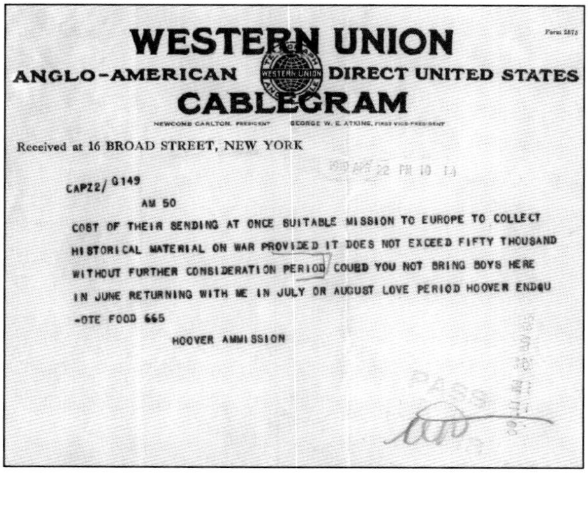

WESTERN UNION

ANGLO-AMERICAN DIRECT UNITED STATES

CABLEGRAM

NEWCOMB CARLTON, PRESIDENT GEORGE W. E. ATKINS, FIRST VICE-PRESIDENT

Received at 16 BROAD STREET, NEW YORK

CAPZ2/ G149

AM 50

COST OF THEIR SENDING AT ONCE SUITABLE MISSION TO EUROPE TO COLLECT HISTORICAL MATERIAL ON WAR PROVIDED IT DOES NOT EXCEED FIFTY THOUSAND WITHOUT FURTHER CONSIDERATION PERIOD COUBD YOU NOT BRING BOYS HERE IN JUNE RETURNING WITH ME IN JULY OR AUGUST LOVE PERIOD HOOVER ENDQU -OTE FOOD 665

HOOVER AMMISSION

At a time when most wealthy Americans favored ornately decorated houses, Lou Henry Hoover designed an innovative home with a surprisingly sleek and modern outline for 1919. Her architect, Birge Clark, credits her directly for the design. Built into a hillside, it is designed to look small and modest from the outside while spacious and light on the inside. Rooftop patios take advantage of the sunny California climate. (SHPC.)

A vintage aerial view of the Lou Henry Hoover House shows how it is situated on San Juan Hill. Both Hoovers had taken an interest in architecture during their years of travel and adventure. Leland Stanford stipulated that the ranchland donated for the university could not be parceled off and sold. The Hoovers built their house on leased property. Today, only faculty and staff may live on campus. (SHPC.)

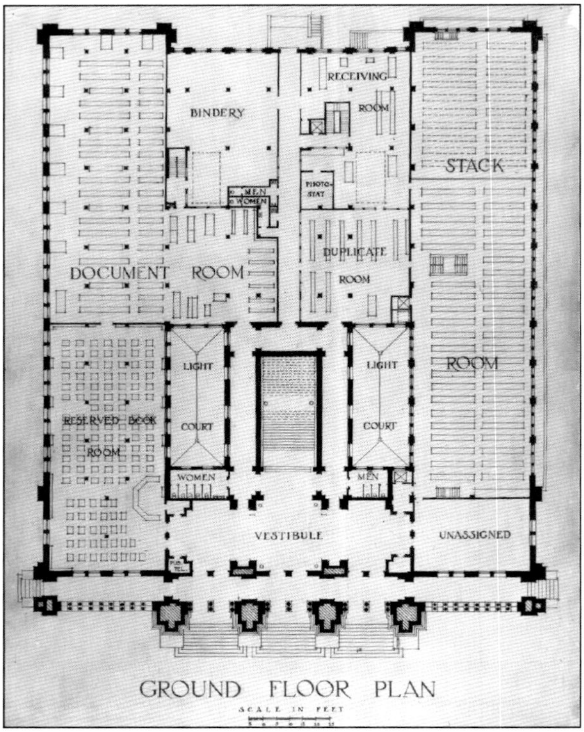

Hoover was asked to clarify the gift of $50,000 ($700,000 in today's money) in the second half of the telegram: "My idea is to simply collect library material on war generally." Professor Adams left for Europe on this mission, exactly a month later, on May 22, 1919. The document storage and the reading room for the new Hoover collection on war and peace had a space just to the right of the main entrance vestibule, an area designated "unassigned" in the ground floor plan. Pictured below, Ralph H. Lutz, left, and Ephraim D. Adams, right, stood by an early shipment to provide a sense of the large scale of the operation. The acquisition of archives may have been innovative for the time, but the plan fit in perfectly with the shared vision of Stanford, White, Jordan, and Branner. (HOOVER.)

Hoover's earlier gifts to the library had been merged with the main university collection. After 1919, when the newly completed university library allowed for more space, Hoover's acquisitions were kept as a separate collection with a specific collecting scope focusing on rare and ephemeral political documents such as propaganda pamphlets. With the large shipments coming in from war-torn Europe, the new space was rapidly outgrown. This vintage photograph shows the original Hoover Library reading room in what is now administrative offices for Green Library and the University Library System. (HOOVER.)

Ralph H. Lutz (1886–1968), a Stanford freshman in 1902, worked as a personal assistant to David Starr Jordan to organize his peace correspondence. Lutz witnessed the 1906 earthquake, the year he graduated. He received a law degree at the University of Washington and a doctorate in history at the University of Heidelberg. Adams recruited him to help Hoover collect documentation on the Great War in 1919. (Stanford University Archives.)

Hoover collector Frank A. Golder (1877–1929) was born in Russia and emigrated to the United States with his family. He conducted research in Russia in 1914, 1917, 1921–1923, 1925, and 1927. He was teaching at Stanford in 1920 when he was recruited to collect documents for Hoover's new program, and he departed on his first collecting trip in August 1920, a trip that lasted three years. (Stanford University Archives.)

Frank Golder entered Soviet Russia affiliated with the American Relief Administration (ARA), Hoover's program to feed the Russians during the famine unleashed by war and revolution. In addition to books, pamphlets, and posters, Golder acquired a unique set of 37 original paintings by the artist Ivan A. Vladimirov, based on the artist's eyewitness drawings of the consequences of the societal collapse. One watercolor depicts once middle-class Russian women and a child scavenging scraps of garbage for food. Another shows a family bringing home food supplies from the ARA on a sled. Because the paintings are critical of the Soviet regime, Golder kept the artist's identity secret. There is a small patch pasted over his signature in many of these paintings. (HOOVER.)

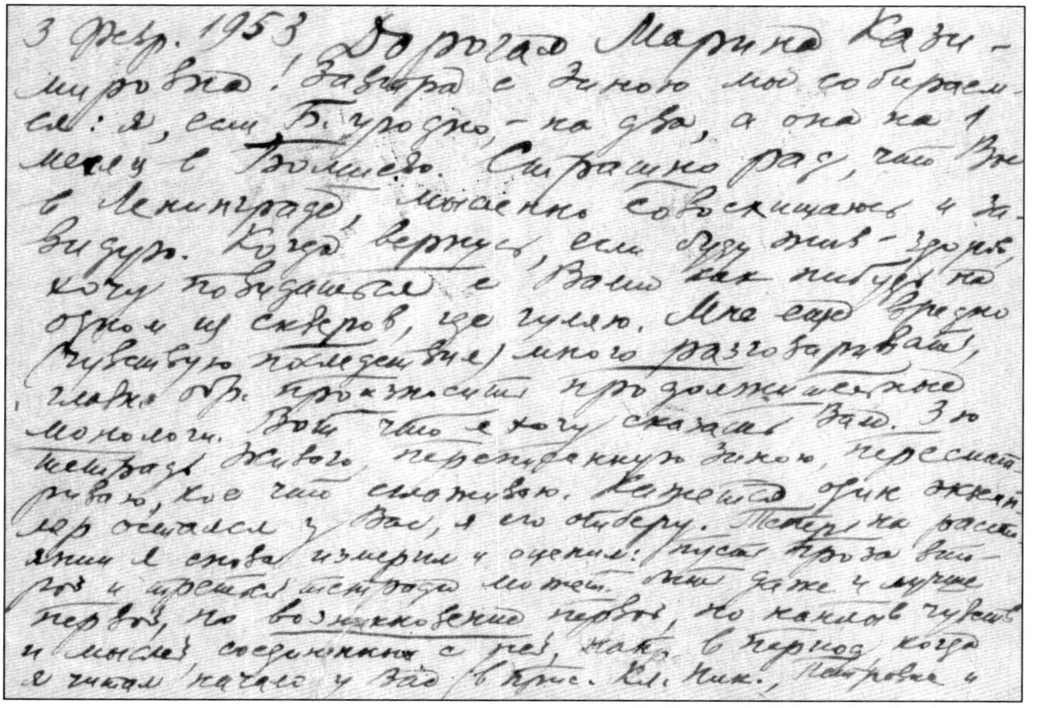

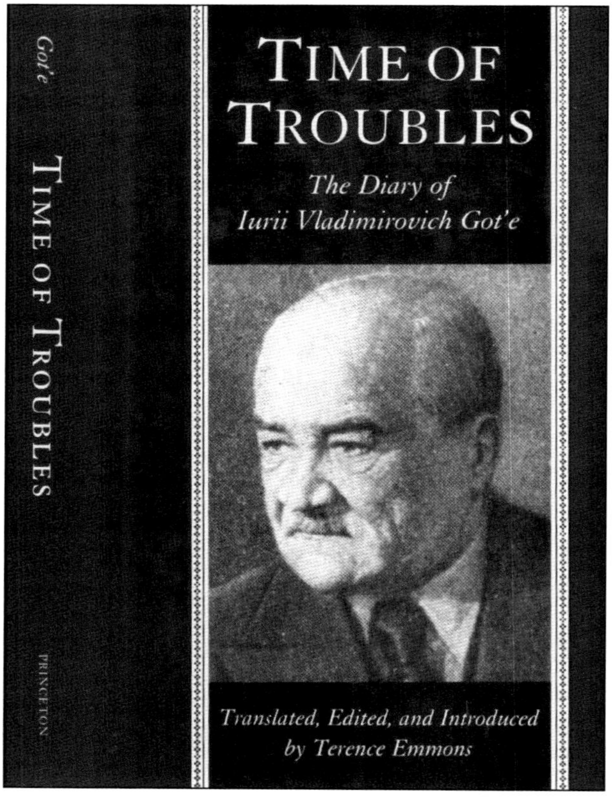

In Russia with Hoover's food relief program, 1921–1923, Golder collected books, journals, and archives on the Russian Revolutions and their tragic aftermath. In 1922, he acquired a handwritten diary for the years 1917–1922, deliberately written by the Russian historian Yurii V. Got'e (Gautier) in Moscow to describe the day-to-day events as a historical document. To protect Got'e from reprisals, Golder kept the name of the author secret. (HOOVER.)

Few such diaries exist, as owning them was dangerous. Golder collected for the future. As he wrote to Lutz from Moscow in 1921, "The scholars of the year 2000 will thank me." The identity of the author was revealed in 1982, long after Golder's death, by Slavic librarian Edward Kasinec. The Got'e diary Golder acquired in 1922 was translated into English and published by Terence Emmons. (R. Danielson.)

In 1918, when Hoover learned about the murder of the Tsar and his family in Ekaterinburg—a city he knew well—he wrote to Frederic R. Coudert that preventing this anarchy from spreading was "the greatest problem our government has ever faced." He saw a clear need to collect original documentation, including this photograph of Tsar Nicholas II and his son Alexei. (HOOVER.)

Lutz was instrumental in acquiring the tsarist secret political police files at the Russian embassy in Paris, a collection known as the "Okhrana," that documents the work of Russian radicals in exile. It includes mug books with images of revolutionaries such as Leon Trotsky. Arriving at Stanford in 1926, the collection was kept secret during the lifetime of the donor, former Russian ambassador to Paris, Vasilii Maklakov. (HOOVER.)

In 1935, Stanford's Western Civilization program included instructors C. Easton Rothwell (director of the Hoover Institution, 1952–1959), Ralph H. Lutz (longtime director of the Hoover library), Harold H. Fisher (also a director), Wallace Sterling (who worked on the Hoover documentary series as a graduate student and later became the fifth president of Stanford University), and Payson J. Treat (who managed Hoover's fund for collecting books on Asia). (Stanford University Archives.)

Nina Almond (1882–1964) was hired by Stanford in 1916, becoming the head librarian for the Hoover collection in 1921. She worked with Ralph Lutz on shipping new materials and editing documentaries. When she retired in 1947, carillonneur James R. Lawson played his own composition "Festive Prelude for Carillon," in honor of Almond, on the bells in the Hoover Tower. (HOOVER.)

A Stanford trustee since 1912, Hoover took an interest in the plans for constructing the Stanford stadium. He was probably not aware that his image, with his iconic stiff collar, would later be featured in a "card trick" at a football game. (SHPC.)

When Hoover was nominated for the presidency by the Republican Party, he officially accepted the nomination in the Stanford football stadium on August 11, 1928, where he was surrounded by tens of thousands of cheering supporters. Here, he is shown arriving at the stadium to make his acceptance speech. (SHPC.)

When Hoover was elected president in November 1928, a crowd assembled on campus, led by the John Philip Sousa band. They marched up to the Lou Henry Hoover House to congratulate the former Stanford student and now president of the United States. The construction of a special Hoover library building would have to wait. (SHPC.)

Three

Construction of Hoover Tower 1939–1941

Starting in 1919, large shipments came in to the Hoover collection in the Stanford Library. Much of the material was in foreign languages and required specialized staff to catalog them. Some of the material, especially from Russia, was restricted for a specific length of time to protect the donors from reprisals and required special handling. The designated space in the university library was soon inadequate. From 1925, the architect, Arthur Brown Jr., was planning to find space for a separate Hoover building.

The university's master plan for the campus, devised by Frederick Law Olmsted and Leland Stanford in 1888, provided space for future construction of matching quadrangles of buildings to the east and west of the historic Main Quad. Brown began an attempt at constructing the corner of a matching sandstone East Quad with the Thomas Welton Stanford Art Gallery, completed in 1917. Further construction was complicated first by the nation's entry into World War I, and later by constrained finances. Hoover was an excellent fundraiser. In 1926, he had raised over half a million dollars to rebuild the Louvain University Library in Belgium after it had been badly damaged by the invading German army. Given his ethical scruples, Hoover postponed raising money for his own library while he was president, and then when the Great Depression hit, the project came to a temporary standstill. Due to financial constraints, the university could not provide more than a small contribution to the total cost of about $600,000 during the Depression, something over $10.3 million in today's dollars.

Not one to be held back for long, Hoover and his trusted associates, such as Edgar Rickard, pulled together $300,000 in funding from the Belgian American Educational Foundation. Residual funds from the American Relief Administration provided an additional $150,000. The Rockefeller Foundation added $50,000. Many small donors, whose names are honored on the walls of the tower lobby contributed the remainder.

Hoover Tower provided a distinct presence for the Hoover Library. The monumental tower design also restored an element to the university as a whole that the founders and pioneers had missed since the earthquake of 1906 brought down the grand, new university library, the Memorial Arch with its observation platform, and the Memorial Church's elegant spire. Ray Lyman Wilbur saw the tower as providing a focal point to the horizontal lines of the university that had been missing for over 30 years.

The modern silhouette of Hoover Tower, completed in 1941, is seen through an ornate sandstone arch from the outer Quad, mainly built in the 1890s. The Thomas Welton Stanford Art Gallery, between the tower and the Quad, was designed by architect Arthur Brown Jr. and completed in 1915 to match the original arcade scheme of the early buildings. With the art gallery, there was an attempt to complete the original Frederick Law Olmsted plan of adding quadrangles to the east and west of the Main Quad. Funding constraints prevented the completion of an East Quad. The university library built in 1919, the School of Education Building built in 1938, and the tower built in 1941 form a cluster rather than a quadrangle. (SHPC.)

Aerial views show the configuration of the Stanford campus before and after the construction of Hoover Tower. In the upper view, the diagonal Palm Drive leads to the grassy Oval in front of the historic Main Quad. The university library and the art gallery, both designed by Arthur Brown Jr., are situated just to the bottom left of the Quad and surrounded by empty fields. The Stanford Stadium, where Hoover accepted the Republican Party's nomination for president in 1928, is the large structure in the lower left quadrant of the photograph. In the image below, a closer view shows the relationship of the tower to the Oval and Quad. (SHPC.)

Arthur Brown Jr. (1874–1957), one of the most prominent and versatile architects of his day, was personally selected by Herbert Hoover to design and build Hoover Tower. Born in Oakland, California, and meticulously trained at the École des Beaux-Arts in Paris, Brown was the architectural genius behind the ornately detailed style of the San Francisco City Hall, completed in 1915. The savvy architect adapted to the modern taste and limited funds of the Depression when, in 1933, he built the sleek, 210-foot-tall, Art Deco Coit Tower on San Francisco's Telegraph Hill. Later, he designed the temporary but majestic 400-foot Tower of the Sun landmark for the 1939 Golden Gate Exposition on Treasure Island. Brown, together with his then-partner John Bakewell, had been designing buildings at Stanford since 1913 and had begun planning the location for the Hoover Library as early as 1925. When funds for the library finally became available, Hoover, a Stanford trustee since 1912, had known Brown for decades. Brown is shown here wearing the heavily embroidered uniform of the Institut de France. (BANCROFT.)

Arthur Brown Jr. sketched these preliminary designs for Hoover Tower, with a squared top. Originally, the reading room had been planned for the top floor to provide a stunning view. Sometime in 1938–1939, he met with Lou and Herbert Hoover at their strikingly modern house on the Stanford campus to discuss the plans. Both Hoovers had a strong interest in architecture. Hoover recalled, "Arthur made the original suggestion that the library building should be a tower for good working purposes. One day he and I were discussing how a tower could fit into the Romanesque motif of the University. Mrs. Hoover suggested that he might find justification in the towers of the Cathedral at Salamanca." The tower acquired a dome. Later, the carillon and observation deck would crown the tower, and the reading room moved to the first floor. (Stanford University Archives.)

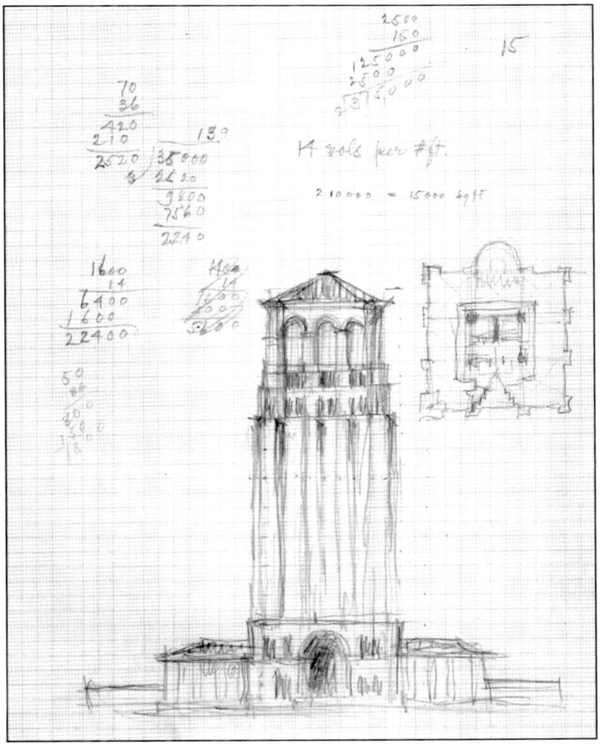

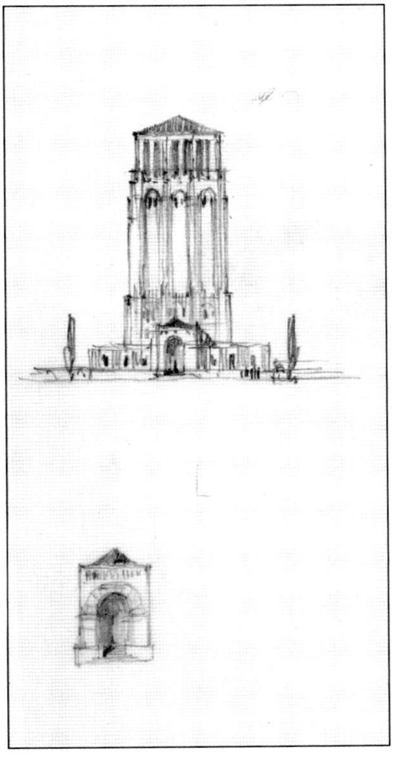

Brown's early designs for the tower have a square roofline. The reading room was originally planned for the top floor, with large windows letting in natural sunlight and opening up a view of the landscape from the foothills to the bay. (HOOVER.)

An early, later revised, cutaway drawing from 1937, signed by the architect, shows the floors devoted to book stacks in a windowless, air-conditioned shaft to protect fragile paper from the damage caused by heat and light. The structure would be a library, a monument, and a viewing platform all in one that would provide a focal point for the low, horizontal lines of the main university buildings. It is designed to withstand earthquakes, as both Hoover and Brown had experienced the rubble left by the 1906 earthquake. (WESTBRANCH.)

Earthquake safety was a major consideration in the construction of Hoover Tower. The original plan for the university included a bell tower rising 80 feet above the roof of the nonsectarian Memorial Church, in a style similar to the Richardsonian Romanesque of Trinity Church in Boston. The spire was said to be modeled on the tower of a cathedral in Salamanca, Spain. The Stanford Memorial Church was dedicated in 1903, and the spire came down just three years later in the 1906 earthquake. Hoover graduated before Memorial Church was built. He saw the earthquake damage in 1909 when he gave a series of lectures, the Principles of Mining, on campus. (SHPC.)

While the church was rebuilt, the spire was never replaced. After the quake, the bells from the spire were originally placed in a wooden tower behind the church and are housed in a small clock tower near the bookstore today. After the 1906 earthquake, the campus took a decade to recover. The rubble was cleared and the campus was mostly rebuilt, but former students who returned to campus, such as Herbert Hoover, Ray Lyman Wilbur, and Ralph Lutz, were very aware of the loss of the earlier magnificent profile of the university. (SHPC.)

Trinity Church, built 1872–1877 in Boston, is considered the masterpiece of architect H.H. Richardson (1838–1886). The Stanfords and Andrew D. White all admired the Richardsonian Romanesque style, which exerted a strong influence on the original campus buildings, although they were designed by a number of different architects. The Hoovers asked that Brown add symbolic elements of Romanesque to the design for the tower's dome. (Division of Rare and Manuscript collections, Cornell University Library.)

A panorama view of campus from across Lake Lagunita shows the original profile of the campus with Memorial Arch on the left and Memorial Church in the center. (SHPC.)

Another loss from the 1906 earthquake, a structure that was never rebuilt, was Memorial Arch, which contained stairs that led up to an observation deck. At 100 feet, it was taller than the surrounding arcades. Stanford president Ray Lyman Wilbur considered rebuilding it, but there was not adequate funding during his presidency (1916–1943). Today, many people feel such an arch would obstruct the view of Memorial Church. (SHPC.)

The 1906 earthquake destroyed the magnificent university library building, not yet completed at the time, which featured an ornate glass dome. Oddly enough, the dome itself initially survived, seen here on the right, but the structure underneath was almost completely demolished. The university library had to remain in inadequate quarters in the Quad until 1919 when Arthur Brown Jr. was able to complete the main library, now known as Green Library Bing Wing. (SHPC.)

The tower was seen by Hoover and Wilbur as restoring an architectural focal point to the horizontal lines of the campus. It was to have an observation platform like Memorial Arch, a bell tower like the original Memorial Church, and a great library. And most of all, it had to be strong and flexible enough to withstand earthquakes. Arthur Brown visited the Hoovers at their campus home to discuss plans in great detail. Brown's 1937 concept of a square roof and his vision reading room with a view were abandoned in order to accommodate a carillon. Hoover suggested that the top of the tower be styled as a dome reminiscent of the bell tower of the Salamanca Cathedral, the model for the lost church spire. While the main architecture is sleek and modern, the dome has Romanesque features. When construction began in 1939, Hoover issued orders to expedite the purchase of the steel I-beams for the frame. With war looming on the horizon, he knew that the price of steel would go up and sources might become scarce. (WESTBRANCH.)

Construction was planned with seismic safety in mind, to the extent possible with the technology of 1939. (SHPC.)

Photographers liked to view the construction through the traditional sandstone arches of the Main Quad. The main university library, now Green Library, can be seen in front of the steel framework. (SHPC.)

This construction shot shows the scaffolding around the tower's steel I-beam frame, again through one of the traditional sandstone arches of the Outer Quad. (SHPC.)

The completed tower framed by the arches with the Romanesque dome was based on the Spanish bell tower in Salamanca. (SHPC.)

Because of the low profile of the Main Quad, the tower dominates views from most directions, seen here from the Quad. (SHPC.)

The observation deck of the Hoover Tower, on the 14th floor, offers stunning views of the sandstone and tile architecture of the historic Main Quad. (SHPC.)

Seen from across Lake Lagunita in a photograph from the 1940s, the university's profile has regained a focal point. The image was captured at Alta Vista, once the residence of university business manager Charles Lathrop, a younger brother of Jane Stanford. Lathrop's three-story mansion was demolished in 1954, and today, the Center for Advanced Study in the Behavioral Sciences occupies the site. (SHPC.)

Four

The Hoover Carillon and Its Renovation 1941 and 2002

When visitors to the 14th-floor observation platform of Hoover Tower exit the elevator, the first thing they see is the 48-bell carillon and a glassed-in room with a keyboard for playing music on the bells. The visitor who turns right and looks up is standing underneath the largest bell, securely fastened to the support structure: it weighs two and a half tons. On special occasions such as commencement, a carillonneur plays concerts in the glass room. While the books and documents preserved in the tower are a great resource for scholars, the carillon is a public instrument, sending out the music for the enjoyment of everyone within range. The current carillon is an expansion of the original set of 35 Belgian bells personally acquired under complex circumstances by Herbert Hoover in 1939–1941.

In 1914, Hoover abandoned his successful international mining career to enter public service with the onset of World War I, when the German army invaded neutral Belgium. Densely populated Belgium depended on imports for three-fourths of its normal food supply, which was abruptly cut off by the invasion. Although the United States was not yet in the war, Hoover felt obligated to help the Belgian people. He organized the Commission for Relief in Belgium (CRB). About 60 mostly unpaid American administrators organized 130,000 volunteers to distribute five million tons of food to see the population through the crisis of the war. While traveling in Belgium, Hoover came to appreciate the consolation of the bells that rang from towers on city halls, churches, and guilds. Since medieval times, the bells have been a symbol of civic liberty.

After the original plans for the Hoover Tower library had been drawn up, Hoover learned that the carillon at the Belgian Pavilion of the New York World's Fair was available for purchase. There were less expensive chimes and carillons available for sale, but for Hoover the symbolism of the Belgian bells was key to the mission of the library. The Latin inscription of the largest "bourdon" bell in the original set reads *una pro pace sono*, or "for peace alone do I ring."

Bronze bells cast by Marcel Michiels of Tournai were installed in the Belgian Pavilion of the New York World's Fair in 1939–1940. A carillon bell does not swing. The keyboard with wooden keys activates wires attached to the clappers to ring each bell manually. Much like a piano, the harder the key is depressed, the louder the sound. The larger bells with clappers are played on foot pedals. (WESTBRANCH.)

The Hoover carillon also has a drum that can automatically play preset melodies by tripping hammers on the outside of each bell as the cylinder rotates. The automatic player mechanism operates much like an oversized music-box cylinder. The pegs can be removed and rearranged to play different melodies. The Hoover automatic player is one of very few its kind in the United States. (WESTBRANCH.)

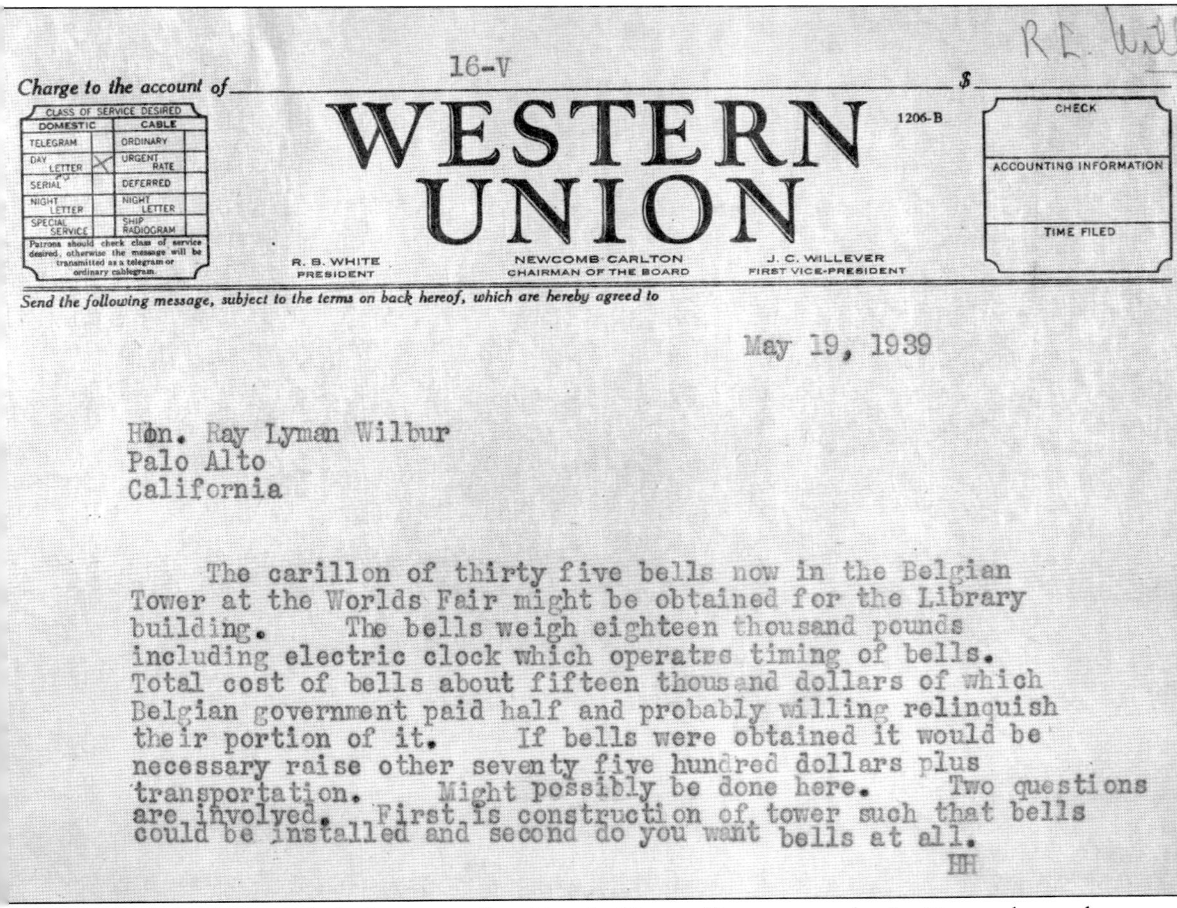

16-V

R.L. Wil

Charge to the account of ______ $ ______

WESTERN UNION

1206-B

CLASS OF SERVICE DESIRED	
DOMESTIC	CABLE
TELEGRAM	ORDINARY
DAY LETTER X	URGENT RATE
SERIAL	DEFERRED
NIGHT LETTER	NIGHT LETTER
SPECIAL SERVICE	SHIP RADIOGRAM

Patrons should check class of service desired, otherwise the message will be transmitted as a telegram or ordinary cablegram.

CHECK

ACCOUNTING INFORMATION

TIME FILED

R. B. WHITE, PRESIDENT — NEWCOMB CARLTON, CHAIRMAN OF THE BOARD — J. C. WILLEVER, FIRST VICE-PRESIDENT

Send the following message, subject to the terms on back hereof, which are hereby agreed to

May 19, 1939

Hon. Ray Lyman Wilbur
Palo Alto
California

The carillon of thirty five bells now in the Belgian Tower at the Worlds Fair might be obtained for the Library building. The bells weigh eighteen thousand pounds including electric clock which operates timing of bells. Total cost of bells about fifteen thousand dollars of which Belgian government paid half and probably willing relinquish their portion of it. If bells were obtained it would be necessary raise other seventy five hundred dollars plus transportation. Might possibly be done here. Two questions are involved. First is construction of tower such that bells could be installed and second do you want bells at all.

HH

May 1939, three months before groundbreaking for Hoover Tower was to begin, Hoover learned of the availability of the Belgian carillon from the New York World's Fair. It would be the perfect symbol of the mission to promote peace. Brown had to reconfigure the top of the tower to support the weight and size of the carillon and adjust the acoustic qualities of the newly designed belfry for the sound to spread out over the campus. Brown asked for diagrams of the bells; none could be found. Hoover had to raise additional funds to pay the Belgian foundry and heavy customs duties. The Belgian carillonneur Kamiel Lefévere was engaged to install the bells with stainless-steel wire to link the clappers and hammers to the clavier and drum. Construction went forward in August before the bells were acquired and funding for the additional expenses had been secured. Between ground breaking in 1939 and the arrival of the Belgian carillon in 1941, overwhelming German military forces had once again invaded Belgium. The symbolism of the carillon became more important than ever. (HOOVER.)

The Belgian American Educational Foundation purchased the carillon. The largest, or "bourdon," bell in the original set from Belgium weighs 1,350 pounds and has the pitch of G-sharp. The full text of the inscription cast into the bronze reads, "Quia Nominor Leopoldus Regius, Una pro pace sono super fluctus Atlantis" (Because I am called Leopold the Royal/ For peace alone do I ring over the waves of the Atlantic). (WESTBRANCH.)

Hoover Library director Ralph Lutz, on the left in an overcoat, inspects the installation of the original carillon bells, which were brought up to the 14th floor of the tower in the main passenger elevator. Using precise measurements, Arthur Brown determined that the 1941 carillon could be installed without the use of cranes. (HOOVER.)

Brown installed the bells prior to laying the travertine floor to avoid marring the finish. The largest bells are lined up in the lobby of Hoover Tower where Hoover Library director Ralph Lutz on the left consults with Stanford Associates public affairs officer Templeton Peck. Peck helped organize the 50th anniversary of the 1891 founding of the university. The carillon concert was a highlight of the celebration. (SHPC.)

Palo Alto historian, Guy Miller, class of 1901, took this now faded snapshot of the installation of the carillon. This wooden beam structure was in use from 1941 until the carillon was renovated in 2000–2002. The workman on the left is unidentified. (SHPC.)

Belgian-born Kamiel Lefévere (1888–1972) was the greatest carillonneur in the United States when the Belgian American Educational Foundation purchased the carillon for the Hoover Tower. Lefévere helped with the purchase negotiations, dismantled the carillon from its temporary installation at the Belgian Pavilion in the New York World's Fair in 1940, reprogrammed the automatic player for American melodies, wired the bells for the belfry of the Hoover Tower in March 1941, and played the first concerts, including the inaugural concert on June 20, 1941. His efforts made the successful operation of the complex carillon mechanism from 1941 to 2002 possible. In 1941, he said, "I hope Stanford eventually can add at least three more heavy bells to its collection." Arthur Brown Jr. ensured that there was space for future additions. In 2002, Lefévere's hopes for an expanded carillon were realized. (Bok Tower Gardens.)

James B. Angell, Stanford professor of electrical engineering (1924–2006), served as university carillonneur from 1960 until 1990. He both maintained and played the instrument on a regular basis; he was at the keyboard at the top of Hoover Tower in 1989 when the Loma Prieta earthquake hit. He was a major force in the campaign to expand and upgrade the instrument. (Chuck Painter/ Stanford News Service.)

Margo Halsted played the carillon for the Stanford commencement in 1965. She was taught by Stanford's official carillonneur Prof. James B. Angell (1924–2006) of the university's Electrical Engineering Department. Here, she is playing the keyboard in its original location on the poorly lighted 13th floor of Hoover Tower, among stacks of library books. Halsted, associate carillonneur at Stanford from 1967–1977, was later instrumental in the renovation of the Stanford carillon in 2000–2002, when the keyboard was moved up to the observation deck. She was a consultant for the expansion of the University of California, Berkeley (UC Berkeley) campanile bells from chimes to a full carillon in 1979 and participated in the project to restore the carillon at the Leuven University Library in Belgium in 1983. The photograph shows the horizontal wooden keys that are pounded to activate the bells. Each key is attached to a wire at the far end that goes up to the next level, where it is attached to a clapper inside the bell. (Chuck Painter/SHPC.)

Carillons are "the symbol of our cherished civic rights and civic liberties" according to Count van der Straten Ponthoz, the Belgian ambassador to the United States in 1939. The use of carillons as a symbol of civic liberty goes back to the 16th century, although the ability to tune them with precision to play melodies dates from the 17th century. The bells announced services, warned of fires, and celebrated victories. In the early-20th century, carillons became popular in the United States. While many of them were placed in churches, college campuses began to construct bell towers as a symbol of academic freedom. Julia Morgan designed a Mission-style bell tower, El Campanil, for Mills College in 1904. The four bells that once hung in the spire on the top of Stanford's memorial church fell in the 1906 earthquake; since 1983, they have been housed in a clock tower near the campus bookstore. The University of California's 307-foot campanile has a carillon of 61 bells. (HOOVER.)

Despite years of successful use, the bells were never quite in tune. In 1943, Ralph Lutz suggested the need to restore them. In 1971, Professor Angell began a campaign to have the bells retuned. Then, in 1996, an engineering student named Nick Merz took an interest and asked Timothy Zerlang, Stanford carillonneur since 1991, about the process. The project was taken up by then Hoover Institution director John Raisian and deputy director Charles G. Palm. In 2000, a Dutch worker dismantled the Hoover bells to ship to the Netherlands for renovation. The original Belgian foundry of Marcel Michiels was no longer in business, but the Dutch foundry of Royal Eijsbouts in Asten took over their business. Eijsbouts retuned the existing Hoover bells and added more, extending the number to 48. (SHPC.)

In 2002, cranes were required to hoist the new, larger carillon into the 14th floor observation deck of Hoover Tower. Facilities coordinator Craig Snarr was in charge of logistics. Of the original 35 bells, 11 had to be replaced. The range was increased by another 13 bells, for a total of 48, to make the carillon a concert instrument of four octaves. Donors of the new bells selected inscriptions to be cast in the bronze, such as "Ring for Freedom" and "Ring for Joy and Peace." (Craig Snarr/HOOVER.)

University carillonneur Timothy Zerlang, who worked with both James Angell and Margo Halsted on expanding and upgrading the Hoover carillon, plays the bells for graduation and other festive occasions. (Above, Craig Snarr/HOOVER; left, Linda A. Cicero/Stanford News Service.)

Five

The Dedication of the Tower and Library 1941

Stanford had much to celebrate in 1941. In the 50 years since its founding, three remarkable presidents—David Starr Jordan, John Casper Branner, and Ray Lyman Wilbur—had navigated the university to success through a financial crisis in 1893, an earthquake in 1906, the repercussions of World War I, and the exigencies of the Great Depression. A benefactor since he had a steady job, alumnus Herbert Hoover sent money, and more importantly advice, to his alma mater. A trustee for 50 years, he worked with the university on finances, faculty salaries, and construction. Already in 1939, a new organization of supporters, the Stanford Associates, began planning for the 50th jubilee. According to Templeton Peck, class of 1929, "A central objective of the Fiftieth Anniversary planners was to bring Stanford forward in the notice of the academic world." In the 1930s, Stanford was not ranked as high as it could or should have been according to reports in the *Atlantic Monthly*. A rigorous academic program was called for to celebrate the golden jubilee. A budget was drawn up to bring leading experts in education from around the country to speak at a four-day symposium, June 16–19, 1941. UC Berkeley physicist Ernest O. Lawrence spoke openly about the potential of nuclear energy, a topic that would soon become top secret. Aurelia Reinhard, president of Mills College, spoke about education for women, a subject of importance to Andrew D. White and Leland Stanford. Other speakers included Lewis Mumford, Edwin P. Hubble of the Mt. Wilson Observatory, Archibald MacLeish, and Stanford alumnus and former president of the United States Herbert Hoover.

Following the symposium, there was an assembly to dedicate the newly constructed Hoover Tower. The shadow of war in 1941 made the discussions all the more serious. Charles Seymour, president of Yale University, said of the Hoover Library, "The significance of the collections here housed cannot be overstated, for they will serve not merely historians but mankind. . . . Only through a knowledge that will guide us to the discovery of a political substitute for war can we hope . . . to control the revolutions that inevitably spring from total war . . . we are all of us under inestimable debt to President Hoover." There were also lighter moments as when the Belgian carillonneur serenaded the crowd with a lively concert on the bells recently installed on the 14th floor of Hoover Tower, and the San Francisco Symphony performed in nearby Frost Amphitheater.

In 1941, the university celebrated its 50th anniversary, the Golden Jubilee. Dedicating the new Hoover Tower was a highlight of the year-long celebrations. The Stanford Choir performed from the observation platform on March 9, 1941, for Founders' Day. Kamiel Lefevere played sunset concerts from the belfry during Commencement Week in June. The tower at night was specially lit with newly developed mercury lighting. (SHPC.)

Hoover's speech from the steps of the tower promised to "dedicate this institution to promote peace." The program was broadcast over radio to a nationwide audience. As secretary of commerce, Hoover had played a key role in the development of radio in the United States. (WESTBRANCH.)

On the afternoon of June 20, 1941, about 2,000 people gathered in front of Hoover Tower for its formal dedication by Herbert Hoover. They are sitting where the fountain is today. (SHPC.)

Charles Seymour, president of Yale University, also spoke, thanking Hoover for this great contribution to scholarship and international understanding. (SHPC.)

On the evening of June 20, 1941, the San Francisco Symphony played a concert for 7,000 guests gathered outside in Frost Amphitheater, with the brightly illuminated Hoover Tower providing light in the background. The celebrated Pierre Monteux, a popular figure on campus, was the conductor of the symphony. (SHPC.)

Standing at the tower's elevator door, under the inscription from Hoover's dedication speech, are Harold H. Fisher (Hoover War Library director), Ray Lyman Wilbur (Stanford University president), Edgar Rickard (president of the Belgian American Educational Foundation), and Herbert Hoover, all looking very serious in 1941. The university went ahead with the 50th jubilee celebrations despite the looming threat of war, but war was on everyone's mind. The library's mission statement had become all the more urgent. (SHPC.)

Hoover is seen here with Harold H. Fisher, director, looking at library acquisitions. They are standing in front of a Belgian tapestry that celebrates Hoover's role in the Commission for Relief Administration. The tapestry was on display at the Belgian Pavilion of the 1939 New York World's Fair and was later donated to the Hoover Institution. The Belgian American Educational Foundation made the construction of Hoover Tower financially feasible. (SHPC.)

Hoover examines a display in the lobby of the tower with his awards and memorabilia from his long career in humanitarian relief programs. These exhibition cases remained in use for 50 years, from 1941 until 1991. (SHPC.)

Hoover spent many hours examining the tower library's historical archives, many of which described events he participated in. Among the Belgian memorabilia for the work of the Commission for Relief in Belgium are stacks of embroidered flour sacks. The American flour was baked into bread for the Belgian children during the German occupation in World War I. Then the empty sacks were decorated by Belgian women with colorful needlework. Here, the sacks are hung in a temporary display in an unfinished basement area of the tower to remind him of this chapter in his life. (SHPC.)

A four-day symposium of nationally recognized leaders in education provided substance to the June 1941 celebrations. This panel on stage in Memorial Auditorium (across from the tower) included Robert Swain, Leland Cutler, Ray Lyman Wilbur, Herbert Hoover, Edgar E. Robinson, Floyd McElroy, and Floyd Parton. (SHPC.)

Three speakers posed in front of Hoover Tower. Physicist Ernest O. Lawrence, to the left, presented a paper on the work to split the atom: "Converting its matter into energy . . . whose possibilities stagger the imagination." Center is Aurelia Henry Reinhardt, president of Mills College, who promoted education for women: "The University must accept women as objectively as men . . . as persons capable of achievement." On the right is chemist Robert E. Swain, master planner for the year-long celebration. (SHPC.)

Lou Henry Hoover was asked to speak at the commencement on June 15, 1941. She joined the procession in academic robes. Her speech recalled "Real adventure . . . in China, Burma, on the deserts and in the mountains of Australia, in New Zealand and Tasmania, on the trails of the Caesars in the Alps and of the Pharaohs across the Red Sea into Arabia, and in the Ural Mountains before 1914." (SHPC.)

Hoover also participated in the October events of 1941, shown here on the Main Quad sitting next to Ray Lyman Wilbur while Leland W. Cutler of the board of trustees addresses the university. (SHPC.)

In October 1941, the celebration continued with a reunion of the pioneer class of 1895, shown here having lunch on the roof of the Lou Henry Hoover House. It is possible to see the Lou Henry Hoover House from the 11th floor of Hoover Tower, where Ray Lyman Wilbur and Hoover had offices. (SHPC.)

Poet, journalist, and radio broadcaster Charles K. Field and his Zeta Psi fraternity brother Shirley Baker, both class of 1895, serenaded the reunion with a rendition of "Out into the Cold, Cold World." Hoover Tower can be seen from the rooftop patio of the Lou Henry Hoover House. (SHPC.)

A fondly remembered highlight of the October 1941 phase of the 50th anniversary celebration took place on the Quad at night, with dancing to the band of Ernest "Ernie" Heckscher, class of 1938. Charles K. Field organized a well-received display of 98 historical slides projected onto the sandstone wall of the Main Quad. The dance was illuminated by newly invented mercury lights shining down from Hoover Tower. (SHPC.)

Ray Lyman Wilbur was persuaded to postpone his retirement as university president in order to preside over the 50th anniversary events. He often talked with students on the Quad. In the background, the main university library from 1919 and the Hoover Tower, completed in 1941, can be seen. Wilbur served as university president until 1943 and then as chancellor until his death in 1949. (SHPC.)

On June 22, 1941, two days after the dedication of the tower, Nazi Germany invaded Russia. And with Pearl Harbor on December 7, 1941, the United States was drawn into World War II. Hoover's staff participated fully in the Army Specialized Training Program on the Stanford campus. The curators applied their experience from World War I to begin documenting the second. (SHPC.)

An inscription in the Hoover Tower lobby, over the gate to the library entrance, reminds visitors that they are entering a library with books and manuscripts on war, revolution, and peace, subjects of importance to the founders of Stanford University. (HOOVER.)

Hoover himself spent many hours studying the documentation in the library. He worked frequently with co-director and legendary library collector Ralph Lutz. They consulted together in the library stacks, which take up most of the space in the tower. In the background are packages of library material waiting to be opened and cataloged for researchers. Lutz edited numerous documentaries. (WESTBRANCH.)

One of the Hoover Library's most devoted readers, Hoover read extensively and wrote thousands of pages of memoirs and commentary. Some of his writing has only recently been published posthumously. Here, he poses in front of a bookcase in Hoover Tower. The top two shelves hold bound transcripts from documentation in the American Relief Administration collection. The third shelf holds documentary publications sponsored by the Hoover Library. (SHPC.)

Student Robert Mallett posed with Hoover's book *Challenge to Liberty* in front of a sculpture of Hoover by California artist Haig Patigian. The bust was donated to the Hoover Library in the 1930s by the widow of T.C.C. Gregory, Hoover's associate with the American Relief Administration in Hungary. The sculpture was relocated to Hoover Tower, where it remains today. (SHPC.)

Hoover, seen here around 1950 in his Hoover Tower office, works on his memoirs with the inspiring view of his beloved campus. Although he lived most of the year in New York, Hoover maintained an office on the 11th floor where he worked summers. (HOOVER.)

Hoover, pictured around 1960 coming out of his office, was surrounded by his memorabilia. To the right of the office door, in the large frame, is an illuminated scroll thanking Hoover for his food relief work in Russia during the famine of 1921–1923. In 1962, when the Herbert Hoover Presidential Library was completed at his birthplace in West Branch, Iowa, his presidential papers and memorabilia such as this scroll were moved from the tower and transferred to the library in Iowa. (HOOVER.)

Originally, a portrait of Hoover by Howard Chandler Christy presided over the main reading room of Hoover Tower on the first floor. The emblem from Hoover's World War I conservation program, the US Food Administration, was hung over the librarian's door. On the right was a Belgian tapestry celebrating Hoover's humanitarian work leading the Commission for Relief in Belgium, with an image of the young robust Hoover. (HOOVER.)

As seen in a photograph from 2017, the Hoover Tower Reading Room is still in active use for research projects, where large windows let in ample natural light. (Alex Shashkevich Stanford News Service.)

Six

Building a Research and Policy Center 1945–2018

Six months after the tower opened, the United States was drawn into World War II. The curators at the Hoover Library were called on to teach classes for the military. Collecting intensified. The need for understanding global politics was no longer theoretical.

In 1945, as the war drew to a close, 50 nations sent 850 delegates and some 3,500 staff members to San Francisco to meet in the War Memorial Opera House, another building designed by Arthur Brown Jr., to draft the Charter of the United Nations (UN). C. Easton Rothwell, the executive secretary of the UN Conference, would become director of the Hoover Library. Witold Sworakowski, who was affiliated with the Polish Delegation, which came later to the conference, would join the staff of the Hoover Library. CBS news coverage included commentary by a former Hoover research associate, Caltech history professor J.E. Wallace Sterling, who would later serve as Stanford's fifth president (1949–1968). The library subject area specialists included Christina Harris for Middle East collections, Mary Wright for the Chinese collections, Ruth Perry for the African collections, and Agnes Peterson for the European collections. A synergy developed among the international visitors, curators, and researchers that continues to this day. Alexander Kerensky, last leader of pre-communist Russia, and later Russian dissident Alexander Solzhenitsyn have had offices in Hoover Tower. The visiting dignitaries from Asia include members of the Chiang Kai-shek family and T.V. Soong family, whose papers are preserved in the Hoover Archives.

Publishing was expanded beginning in 1960 with the directorship of W. Glenn Campbell, who developed an innovative policy research program. Campbell brought luminaries such as Nobel Prize–winning economist Milton Friedman to the Hoover Institution, which has become increasingly influential in public policy matters. The next major challenge was documenting the collapse of communism in Germany in 1989 and the Soviet Union in 1991. Documenting the post-communist turmoil has been an even greater challenge. The collections continue to grow. The research fellows publish their findings on a broad array of economic and political issues.

Many of the delegates from the UN Conference in 1945 made their way from San Francisco to Stanford, and the tower was the natural place to meet with Americans interested in international relations. One visitor was Prince Faisal bin Abdulassis, later King Faisal of Saudi Arabia, seen here with his entourage being greeted by library director Harold H. Fisher. Fisher provided Prince Faisal with a display of selected Middle East materials from the collection. Documentary exhibits for foreign visitors would become a major activity for the Hoover Library & Archives. (SHPC.)

Members of the Iraqi delegation also made their way to Hoover Tower: Abdul Jabbar Chalabi, Fadhil Al-Jamali, Majid Kheduri, and Abdul Majid Abbas. (SHPC.)

Christina Harris, seen here with her husband, Stanford historian David Harris, served as the Middle East curator for the Hoover Library. Exceptionally knowledgeable, she collected materials that would later provide rare insights into Middle East politics, such as documentation on the origins of the Muslim Brotherhood. (SHPC.)

Journalists also came to the tower during the UN Conference such as Mrs. Albert C. Lim, Hu Lin, and Hsiao Chien, representatives of the Chinese press. Rotating exhibits in the lobby brought the holdings of the library to the attention of such visitors, another tradition that continues today with an active exhibition program. (SHPC.)

Mary Wright, pictured at right, was the first curator for the Chinese collection. She arranged for large shipments of library materials from China at the end of World War II. She supervised the unpacking and sorting of the materials with then-director Easton Rothwell. (HOOVER.)

Members of the Indian delegation to the U.N. Conference enjoyed the view from the observation deck of Hoover Tower: K.P. Thampi; Mrs. J.A. Kilalee of Burlingame, California; and K.A. Khan. The waist-high railing on the platform openings seen here has since been replaced with a complete grid for safety reasons. (SHPC.)

Members of the Guatemalan delegation rested on the bench in the tower lobby: Julio Bonilla Gonzalez, Manuel Noriega Morales, Gabriel Biguria, Mrs. Biguria, and Jose Luis Mendoza. The wall behind them bears the names of the many donors required to fund construction of Hoover Tower. (SHPC.)

Curator Ruth Perry expanded the Hoover's African holdings. The collecting began in 1919 with materials given to Hoover by Belgium on the history of the Belgian Congo. In the 1920s, Nina Almond added more materials from the League of Nations. (SHPC.)

Seen here in the lobby, Taha Elsayed Nasr, legal advisor to the government of Egypt during the UN Conference, also visited the tower. There are frequently still long lines of visitors and tourists waiting to use the elevator to the observation platform. (SHPC.)

Members of the Philippine delegation included Col. Alejandro Melchor, and Vincente G. Sinco, posing in front of the sculpture of Herbert Hoover by Haig Patigian. On the wall hung a Belgian tapestry that was made for the Belgian Pavilion of the 1939 New York World's Fair. (SHPC.)

High-level dignitaries continued to visit Hoover Tower, such as Elpidio Quirino, president of the Philippines, who conferred with Hoover Library director Harold H. Fisher in 1949. (SHPC.)

Stojan Gavrilovich, undersecretary of state for foreign affairs of Yugoslavia and deputy delegate to the UN Conference conferred with library director Ralph Lutz in front of the Hoover Library. Like many visitors who viewed the library holdings, he began to contribute materials and was recruited as a part-time collector. (SHPC.)

This rare poster depicts a battle from the Chinese revolution of 1911 that overthrew thousands of years of the Chinese empire and established a republic. In 1911, Lou and Herbert Hoover were living in London but they followed events with great interest because of their experiences in the Boxer Rebellion 10 years earlier. (HOOVER.)

The Hoover Archives preserves original materials on Sun Yat-sen, the leader of the 1911 revolution, including vintage photographs such as this one. (HOOVER.)

Journalist Helen Foster Snow donated her papers on China, including this photograph from her meeting with a young Mao Zedong (on the right) from the time that she interviewed him in Yenan in 1937. (HOOVER.)

The Hoover Archives poster collection, which holds an estimated 100,000 original historical broadsides, many in full color, is one of the most heavily used of all the collections. A poster of Mao shows how his little red book was used by the crowds as a symbol of the Cultural Revolution. (HOOVER.)

The curators try to document all sides of political conflicts. Here, Gen. Chiang Kai-shek, Madame Chiang, and Gen. Joseph Stilwell enjoy a rare moment of congeniality in a conflicted relationship between the Chinese and American generals that complicated the conduct of World War II in Asia. The Hoover Archives hold the original handwritten wartime diaries of General Stilwell. The hand-calligraphed diaries of Chiang Kai-shek were placed in the Hoover Archives on deposit in 2004. Both collections are open to the public for research and provide very different perspectives on the Chinese experience in the war. (HOOVER.)

An important researcher at the Hoover Library was Alexander Kerensky (1881–1970), a highly influential Russian politician during the early 20th century and the last prime minister of Russia before Lenin came to power. Kerensky came to visit the Russian collections in 1955 and forged an 11-year association with the library and the university. In the image above, he is shown on the right, with Hoover associate director Witold Sworakowski (1903–1979). Kerensky edited, with Robert Browder, a documentary on the Russian Provisional Government, combining his personal knowledge and the documents collected by the library. The volume was published as a Hoover Institution Publication by the Stanford University Press in 1961. Kerensky, who had an office in Hoover Tower, taught formal classes in Russian history and generously held informal discussions with students that have become legendary. (HOOVER.)

In 1957, files of the tsarist secret political police, the Okhrana, could finally be unsealed. The collection was acquired in 1926 from the tsarist embassy in Paris and kept secret for over 30 years. Once the tower was completed, the crates were moved to the top floor. One publicity photograph from the opening of the papers shows Witold Sworakowski sorting files with librarian Marina Tinkoff. In another, Sworakowski, on the right, examines the papers with Easton Rothwell, who served as director of the Hoover Institution from 1952 to 1959, on the left. (In 1945, both Sworakowski and Rothwell had worked at the UN Conference in San Francisco.) The Okhrana collection holds police dossiers on revolutionaries such as Trotsky, Lenin, and Stalin, as well as hundreds of lesser known figures. It remains a major primary source for the study of the Russian Revolution. (HOOVER.)

The Russian poster collection is notable for rare items such as this lithographed World War I poster drawn by Leonid Pasternak, father of Nobel Prize winning novelist Boris Pasternak. The poster was sold to raise money for the wounded in the tragic conflict that would eventually bring down the tsarist regime. The last tsar, Nicholas II, objected to the poster because it made the Russian soldier look weak. The Bolsheviks repurposed the image in a campaign to withdraw from the conflict, using the drawing without permission from the artist. (HOOVER.)

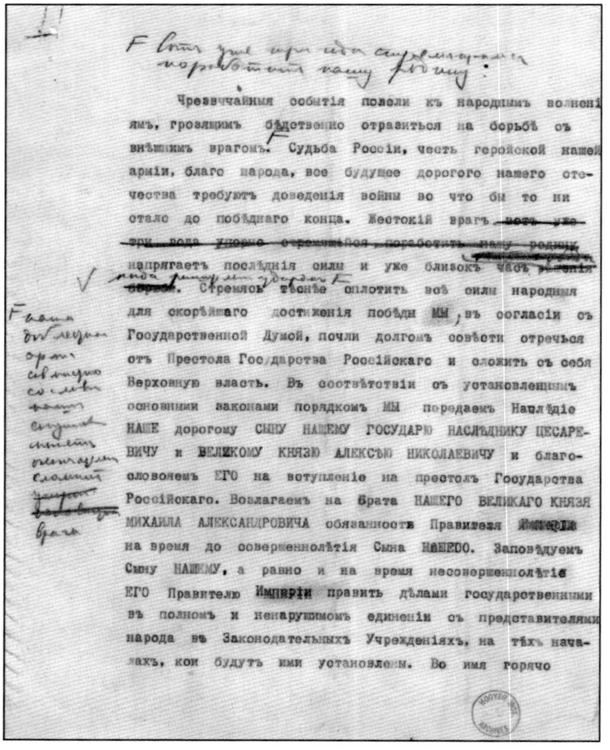

Чрезвычайныя событія повели къ народнымъ волненіямъ, грозящимъ бѣдственно отразиться на борьбѣ съ внѣшнимъ врагомъ. Судьба Россіи, честь геройской нашей арміи, благо народа, все будущее дорогого нашего отечества требуютъ доведенія войны во что бы то ни стало до побѣднаго конца. Жестокій врагъ напрягаетъ послѣднія силы и уже близокъ часъ. Стремясь тѣснѣе сплотить всѣ силы народныя для скорѣйшаго достиженія побѣды МЫ, въ согласіи съ Государственной Думой, почли долгомъ совѣсти отречься отъ Престола Государства Россійскаго и сложить съ себя Верховную власть. Въ соотвѣтствіи съ установленнымъ основными законами порядкомъ МЫ передаемъ Наслѣдіе НАШЕ дорогому СЫНУ НАШЕМУ ГОСУДАРЮ НАСЛѢДНИКУ ЦЕСАРЕВИЧУ и ВЕЛИКОМУ КНЯЗЮ АЛЕКСѢЮ НИКОЛАЕВИЧУ и благословляемъ ЕГО на вступленіе на престолъ Государства Россійскаго. Возлагаемъ на брата НАШЕГО ВЕЛИКАГО КНЯЗЯ МИХАИЛА АЛЕКСАНДРОВИЧА обязанности Правителя Имперіи на время до совершеннолѣтія Сына НАШЕГО. Заповѣдуемъ Сыну НАШЕМУ, а равно и на время несовершеннолѣтія ЕГО Правителю Имперіи править дѣлами государственными въ полномъ и ненарушимомъ единеніи съ представителями народа въ Законодательныхъ Учрежденіяхъ, на тѣхъ началахъ, кои будутъ ими установлены. Во имя горячо

The papers of Nicolas DeBasily record the tragic events as revolution overwhelmed Russia during World War I. DeBasily was a lawyer tasked with drafting the abdication statement for Tsar Nicholas II in 1917. The original two-page typed draft is in the collection. The last sentence reads, "God save Russia." (HOOVER.)

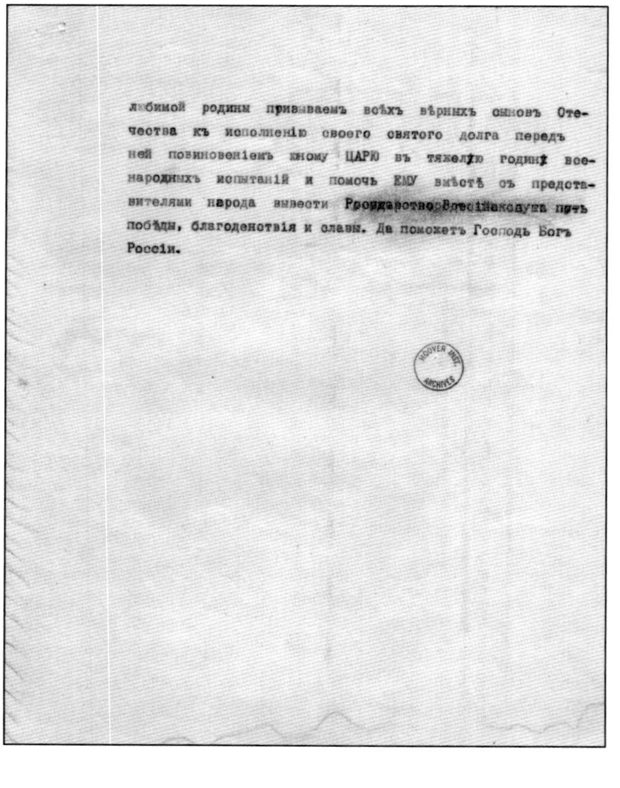

любимой родины призываемъ всѣхъ вѣрныхъ сыновъ Отечества къ исполненію своего святого долга передъ ней повиновеніемъ юному ЦАРЮ въ тяжелую годину всенародныхъ испытаній и помочь ЕМУ вмѣстѣ съ представителями народа вывести [illegible] путь побѣды, благоденствія и славы. Да поможетъ Господь Богъ Россіи.

After donating her late husband's papers and library, Lascelle DeBasily decided to donate his fine art collection as well, which includes oil paintings, primarily portraits of Russian aristocrats. To honor Nicolas DeBasily, the artwork was arranged in a room used for receiving distinguished visitors. (HOOVER.)

The archives collect in all media. The Herman Axelbank collection contains Russian film footage from the tsarist era to Lenin and Stalin. It is a widely used resource. (HOOVER.)

The photographs in the Hoover Archives are just as valuable as the text documents. This image captures Joseph Stalin concluding the 1939 non-aggression treaty with Nazi foreign minister Joachim von Ribbentrop. Stalin's critics were dealt with harshly. Alexander Solzhenitsyn was arrested for criticizing Stalin's conduct of the war and sent to the Gulag, which he describes in his novel *The Gulag Archipelago.* (HOOVER.)

Nobel Prize–winning Russian dissident writer Alexander Solzhenitsyn visited the Hoover Institution in 1975. Senior fellow Richard Staar, on the left, served as his interpreter, both seen here on the steps of Hoover Tower. Solzhenitsyn had an office on the 11th floor, where he studied the Hoover Library's historical Russian newspaper collection to reconstruct the events of World War I, the Russian Revolution, and Civil War. (HOOVER.)

Hoover Institution librarians Phil MacLean and Arline Paul examine incoming materials on Germany in World War II. (HOOVER.)

The Hoover Tower is filled with 17 levels of book stacks. Extra provisions have been installed to protect especially rare items. Agnes Peterson (1923–2008), the curator for the Western European Collections, is shown opening the vault gates to the rare book collection in 1957. She served as reference librarian and curator of the Western European collections from 1952 until 1993. Her work with Ralph H. Lutz, founding co-director of the Hoover Library, ensured a chain of continuity with the very origins of the library. With the fall of communism, she collected ephemeral materials on the unification of Germany. She is shown here with Russian curator Joseph Dwyer. (HOOVER.)

On December 2, 1970, a bolt of lightning hit Hoover Tower during a thunderstorm. It dislodged the 300-pound, concrete ball that sat atop the dome. The ball was still in place in the 1960s. Large pieces of the ball were preserved and labelled by the library staff. (SHPC.)

Over the years, the dome suffered water damage and discoloration in addition to the loss of the ball. For some 25 years, a metal spike protruded from the spot where the ball had been dislodged. (HOOVER.)

In 1995, engineers began restoration work on the tower. They asked to see the fragments preserved by the librarians. From the curvature of the remaining chunks, the engineers were able to calculate the correct size of the ball, which was restored by means of a large crane. (HOOVER.)

The mission statement, as articulated by Herbert Hoover June 20, 1941, still sets the tone for the work of the entire library and public policy center. (HOOVER/Tim Griffith.)

Seven

A Legacy with a Future 1919–2019 and Beyond

The year 2019 marks the centennial of the Hoover Institution, a hundred years since Herbert Hoover sent a telegram to Stanford in 1919 promising $50,000 for a library on the causes of war, revolution and peace. Hoover began collecting books and funding acquisitions for Stanford over a decade earlier, but the Hoover War Collection became a distinct entity in that year. Hoover's own presidential papers were transferred from Hoover Tower to the Herbert Hoover Presidential Library at his birthplace in West Branch, Iowa, in 1962. Hoover's papers from his humanitarian relief programs still reside at Stanford. Since 2001, the Hoover Library & Archives focus only on rare books and archival materials. The university library has assumed the responsibility for the acquisition of standard press books.

The origins of the research program go back to the founding of the university itself with Leland Stanford's speech in 1891 about the benefits of education for building stability in the world. It was an idea with traction. The public policy center at the Hoover Institution is considered one of the finest in the country. There are over a hundred research fellows and senior research fellows, including distinguished public servants such as former secretary of state George P. Shultz, former secretary of defense William J. Perry and former secretary of state Condoleezza Rice. International visitors continue to participate in the work of the Hoover Institution. The late British prime minister Margaret Thatcher was a welcome visitor and honorary fellow. Late director W. Glenn Campbell developed the Hoover Institution Press as a major publisher on policy issues, and the current director, Thomas Gilligan, has continued to expand the reach of the Hoover publications and internet presence.

The past hundred years may have seen dramatic changes, but the core mission of the Hoover Institution has remained the same: document-based policy research on crucial political and economic issues in both the domestic and international arenas.

In the 1980s, the Honorable George P. Shultz, former secretary of state, and Mrs. "Obie" Shultz met for discussions in the DeBasily Room of Hoover Tower with senior fellow Rita Ricardo Campbell and W. Glen Campbell (1924–2001), director of the Hoover Institution from 1960 to 1989. In the background is an 18th-century portrait of Elena Kurakina by artist Dmitry Levitzky, from the DeBasily collection. (HOOVER.)

The Hoover Institution has enjoyed the privilege of hosting numerous world leaders. John Raisian, director of the Hoover Institution from 1989 to 2015, and research fellow Robert Conquest, a British historian and poet, met with Margaret Thatcher, prime minister of the United Kingdom, in 1993. Thatcher (1925–2013) was an honorary fellow of the Hoover Institution. (HOOVER.)

The eminent philosopher Sir Karl Popper (1902–1994), known for his 1945 groundbreaking work, *The Open Society and Its Enemies*, was a senior research fellow at the Hoover Institution. This c. 1930 photograph shows him as a young student in his native Vienna. His papers comprise over 500 manuscript boxes in the Hoover Library & Archives. (HOOVER.)

Seen here at a birthday celebration, the Nobel Prize–winning economist Milton Friedman served as a senior research fellow at the Hoover Institution from 1977 until his death in 2006. His papers comprise more than 200 boxes in the Hoover Library & Archives. (HOOVER.)

When then Soviet president Mikhail Gorbachev visited Stanford in 1990, former secretary of state George Shultz honored his policy of *glasnost* by giving him a duplicate 1921 literacy poster from the Hoover Archives with a quote from Pushkin celebrating the dawn of enlightenment. Gorbachev returned in 1992 and toured the Russian collections of the Hoover Library & Archives. (HOOVER.)

With the collapse of communism in the Soviet Union, Hoover deputy director Charles G. Palm negotiated a microfilm exchange in 1991 with the former Soviet Archives in a historic collaborative project. Hoover preservation officer Judith Fortson and Palm examined some of the 10,000 reels of once secret Soviet documentation. (HOOVER.)

Eric T. Wakin, deputy director of the Hoover Institution and Robert H. Malott Director of the Hoover Institution Library & Archives, has reinvigorated the archives' tradition of innovative collecting while moving forward with digital initiatives. (HOOVER.)

The lobby of Hoover Tower received an upgrade in 1991 for its 50th anniversary. A custom-made reception desk was installed to facilitate the work of the guides who take thousands of visitors up to the observation deck each year. (HOOVER/Tim Griffith.)

Tanner Fountain was completed in 1978 between Hoover Tower and Memorial Auditorium, where cars once parked. Now, only buses and service vehicles are allowed. (HOOVER/Tim Griffith.)

Arthur Brown Jr. paid great attention to the position of the tower relative to the other buildings around it. It sets off the Thomas Welton Stanford Art Gallery, completed by the firm Bakewell and Brown in 1917. The gallery was renovated in 2000 to repair earthquake damage and to bring it back closer to its original architectural plan. (HOOVER/Tim Griffith.)

As intended by Brown, Hoover, and Wilbur, the tower still provides a vertical counterpoint to the front of the Main Quad. The front of the Quad was restored in 2013 to replace statues of Johannes Gutenberg and Benjamin Franklin that went missing from their perches on the façade in about 1949 during an earlier remodeling. (HOOVER/Tim Griffith.)

From 2006 to 2014, the university built the Science and Engineering Quad to the west of the campus core. It is based on Olmsted and Stanford's quadrangle concept, reinterpreted with modern materials and design. Looking east, the Hoover Tower provides a visual anchor for the horizontal lines of the new technology buildings, readily identifiable as Stanford University. (Chor Seng Tan.)

Economist Thomas W. Gilligan, seen here in the reading room of Hoover Tower, assumed the role of the Tad and Dianne Taube Director of the Hoover Institution in September 2015. (HOOVER/Tim Griffith.)

On October 22, 2017, the Hoover Institution opened its fourth building, the David and Joan Traitel Building, to the west of the tower between the art gallery and Green Library. While the tower primarily provides library stacks and the Herbert Hoover and Lou Henry Hoover buildings provide offices, the Traitel Building opens up additional space for conferences and meetings. (HOOVER/Tim Griffith.)

Bibliography

Almond, Nina, and Harold H. Fisher. *Special Collections in the Hoover Library on War, Revolution and Peace*. Stanford: Stanford University Press, 1940

Burdick, Charles B. *Ralph H. Lutz and the Hoover Institution*. Stanford: Hoover Institution Press, 1974.

Danielson, Elena S. *For Peace Alone Do I Ring*. Stanford: Hoover Institution, 2002, reprinted 2017.

Duignan, Peter, editor. *The Library of the Hoover Institution on War, Revolution and Peace*. Stanford: Hoover Institution, 1985.

Fisher, Harold H. *A Tower to Peace: The Story of the Hoover Library on War, Revolution and Peace*. Stanford: Stanford University Press, 1945.

Golder, Frank A. *War, Revolution, and Peace in Russia: The Passages of Frank Golder, 1914–1927*, compiled, edited, and introduced by Terence Emmons and Bertrand M. Patenaude. Stanford: Hoover Institution Press, 1992.

Joncas, Richard, David J. Newman, and Paul Venable Turner. *Stanford University: An Architectural Tour*. New York: Princeton Architectural Press, 2006.

Mirrielees, Edith. *Stanford: The Story of a University*. New York: Putnam, 1959.

Nash, George H. *Herbert Hoover and Stanford University*. Stanford: Hoover Institution Press, 1988.

Nash, George H. *The Life of Herbert Hoover*, vol. 1–3. New York: Norton, 1983, 1988, 1996.

Patenaude, Bertrand M. *A Wealth of Ideas: Revelations from the Hoover Institution Archives*. Stanford: Stanford University Press, 2006.

Peck, Templeton. *When We Were Fifty: The Story of Stanford's Golden Jubilee*. Stanford: Stanford Historical Society, 1985.

Tilman, Jeffrey T. *Arthur Brown Jr.: Progressive Classicist*. New York: Norton, 2006.

Turner, Paul V., Marcia E. Vetrocq, and Karen Weitze. *The Founders & the Architects: The Design of Stanford University*. Stanford: Department of Art, Stanford University, 1976

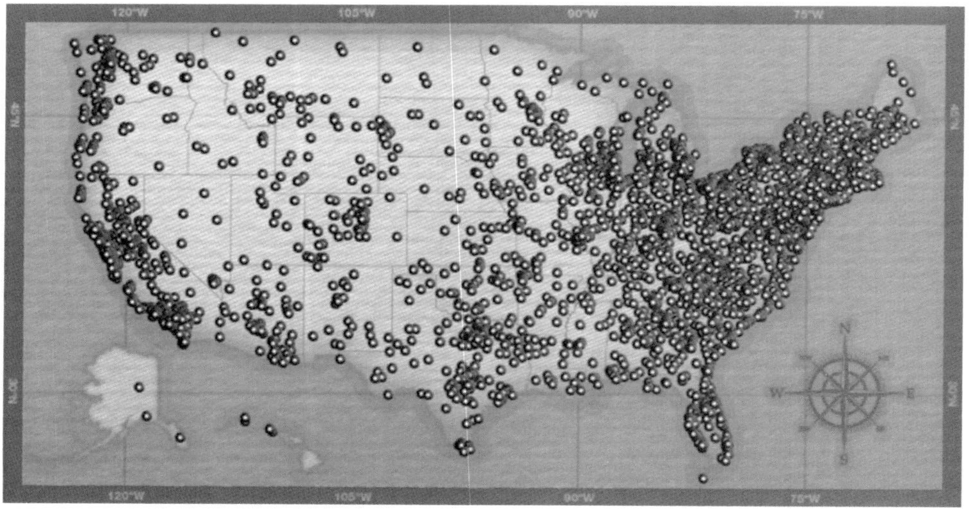